BENJAMIN DUNKS

Intimacy

A guide for young men about sex

Contents

1

Part 1

2

Introduction

This is a book for young men. Guys, you have been abandoned. At one of the most crucial times in your lives, particularly your sexual lives, society, probably your parents and the education system have all abandoned you.

At a time in your life where clear, unapologetic, straight speaking guidance is more important than ever before, when you are desperate for someone to give you information that will help you in your sexual futures, everyone has gone silent.

Except for porn. Porn is there, supposedly telling you everything about sex. Alongside porn are the voices in the world shaming you for watching it, shaming you for trying to relate to it and shaming you for using it as your guide in your sexual futures.

(Part of the reason the people behind these voices are shaming you about watching porn is they are embarrassed about the fact they have abandoned you and they watch porn too.)

Making this worse is a high proportion of women of all ages who have history of sexual assaults by men, deep set issues of sexual assaults in schools and universities, and numerous high profile males being convicted of historic sexual assaults across the globe. The outcome of this is a significant part of the media is saying you are all sexual predators in waiting. You know this isn't the case. I know this isn't the case. Yes, there are some amongst you who will be, but the vast majority of you aren't.

This book is your light in the darkness, the guidance no-one else is giving you. This book is an attempt to fill the void left by everyone else, an attempt to begin to give you answers to questions you will have about sex, about how it happens, about how to be a fantastic partner in an intimate encounter and how to prepare yourself for that encounter.

The idea of this book is simple.

1. You need more information about the actual reality of having sex with someone. This book will give it to you.
2. You need information that won't be shaming. You will not be shamed in this book.
3. You need straight talking knowledge about the reality of sex. You will get that from this book.
4. You need to know that you have a wonderful sexual life ahead of you, and you shouldn't be worried about that. This book will make sure you are in safe hands.

For context, this book was written by a heterosexual, cis-gendered white male, and the experience and life as defined by that is the context by which it has been written.

3

Two Halves

This book is in two halves. The first half has short chapters about sex, about elements of sex you might not know about, you might know a lot about, or you might never have thought about. A lot of these chapters are about things no-one talks about. The second half consists of steps and actions on how to have great sex. These all focus on how to give your partner an extraordinary time in bed,how to create incredible intimate experiences between you and exercises that will help you develop the skills to be able to do this.

The first part is very different to the second. This is deliberate and is meant to give each part the feel of being a book in itself. The main difference is that each of the chapters in the first part can be read by themselves as ideas. So if you want to, you can open a page at random and go from there. In the the second part, the chapters are longer and with a range of elements to them and it will make more sense to read from the start through to the end.

Please don't read part 2 before part 1. Part 1 will give you all the information you need before you dive in to part 2.

4

Actual knowledge about how to have really good sex is hard to come by.

You are all told the basics of sex: how it happens, what to do, how to stay safe, how not to get someone pregnant.

But you aren't told how to have really good sex. No-one tells you this because they are afraid if you realise how amazing really good sex is, you will spend your life rutting like rabbits and there will an epidemic of STD's and an incredible surge in pregnant teenagers. I don't think this will happen.

This book will show you how to have really good sex. It will give you instructions on how to touch your partner in ways that will thrill her and you. It will give you instructions on how to gain sensitivity in your hands so you are able to touch your partner in this way. And it will give you a range of different ideas on all the elements of sex you might have questions about.

It is my belief that if your focus in your sexual encounters is on supporting your partner in having an incredible time, and the experience is one of partnership and not one 'servicing' the other, then you will be laying the foundations for increasingly mind-blowing sexual experiences for the rest of your life.

One of the other main impacts of a population of young men focusing on their partner's pleasure will be a significant decrease in sexual assaults on women.

A lot of these assaults are a result of education by porn. This essentially means guys are watching porn and then emulating what is going on in the porn they see. What they don't understand is this isn't the way sex is in real life and the normalised physicality of porn is closer to what sexual assault is, rather than what real sex is.

A lot of young men understand this isn't the way sex really is, but the power of porn can often override this.

Fantastic real sex is a partnership, not a one way focused event and doesn't involve the kind of activities you see in porn. Sometimes it does but only when it is consensual. This is where the abandonment of you all comes in. If society wasn't so embarrassed about talking about sex, then you would all know this. But because you are left in the dark, the only education you are getting is one teaching you the wrong things.

This doesn't stop you being responsible for your actions.

It is up to you to take responsibility for what you do when you are being intimate with someone. I am not shaming you here either. I am on your side and I want you all to be having the most amazing sex you can be having, when you have it. Focus on your partner and focus on how you can work with your partner to have an extraordinary time.

5

Why aren't we all taught how to have amazing sex?

Why aren't we all taught how to have really fantastic sex? Why isn't it normal everyone across the world just has great sex as part of every experience of sex they have?

This is thoroughly confusing. We are inundated with sex in film, sex on television, sex online, sex in books, sex everywhere. Alongside this the world is experiencing a crisis in our society where a majority of women report sexual assault at least once in their lives, and for many, multiple times.

So we have a situation where we are surrounded by sex as a goal to get to, an incredible and astonishing experience to share with someone you love or fancy, yet on the other hand half our population are experiencing or expecting to experience violence and focused while engaging in the very act that is supposed to be so pleasurable. Finally, those perpetuating these assaults, the males in the other half of the sexual experience, mostly aren't being held to account for it.

So the truly confusing thing here is this. Sex is amazing. Sex is exquisite and intimate and liberating and extraordinary, and with communication and a desire to share these moments of intimacy with someone you fancy and care about it should be all of these things to all of you involved, every time you experience it. So there really should be no reason for assaults to happen, if the focus of sexual encounters is to have a mind-blowing experience every time you do it.

So this is where this book comes in.

Because when you are young and learning about sex no-one talks to you about how fantastic it is. Everyone just tells you not to do it because pregnancy happens and sexually transmitted infections get shared etc... Just the usual fear based 'Don't do it!'. This approach has a great deal of legitimacy, because unwanted pregnancy and sexually transmitted diseases should be actioned against.

But what should also be taught is how to have great sex. What do you do? How do you do it? What do all the wondrous parts of your partner feel like and how do you bring her to the most incredible experience every time you are together?

We should all be having amazing sex. There shouldn't be all these forums online of women talking about how appalling the majority of their sex life is, where no-one they are intimate with knows what they are doing, or are essentially assaulting them because porn has taught them that is how sex happens.

By the end of this book, you will understand how you can have amazing sex all the time. It is within your grasp.

6

Sex and the reality of Intimacy

7

What do you do when you are having sex with someone?

'What do you do when you are having sex with someone?' This is a question everyone asks themselves at some point. What do you do? This book answers this question.

There may well be many of you reading this who have plenty of experience of sex, so your question might be, 'how do I make the whole experience of sex better for my partner and me?'. This question is also answered throughout this book.

The reality is no-one teaches you about what to do with your partner that will result in extraordinary and mind-blowing and amazing sex.

Some of the assumptions about sex go a bit like 'Stick it in, pump a bit, blow your load.' or 'she'll suck me off then I can cum on her face like a porn star', or maybe a combination of both.' These are the most basic ideas of sex, and they don't have any element of intimacy attached to them. And what we are exploring here is intimacy and how to find the most extraordinary pleasure with your partner.

Others will follow the line of, 'I know there are bits and

pieces I can touch that will do wonderful things for her, but I don't know how to make it happen and I don't want to make a mistake.' This line of thinking will lead you closer to intimacy, you just have to move past worrying about making a mistake.

Remember, the (mostly) misogynistic, often violent and aggressive examples of sex in porn is not the way amazing sex happens in reality. It is a fantasy created for men to wank over and to get those men to spend money on watching it. It is about power, about demonstrating power over women and that that kind of power is what is important to men.

The reality of sex in the real world is very different to this. This isn't to say sometimes those power games aren't consensually played and can be great fun for all involved, it is just mostly the sex the majority of people want in the real world experience doesn't involve getting slapped or strangled, doesn't involve being aggressively told what to do and how to do it, doesn't involve deep throating you every time she gives you head, doesn't involve most of the potentially 'extreme' things you might be watching. It might involve some of this sometimes, but not very often and only with consent.

Having amazing sex in the real world involves sharing yourself with someone else and working to make sure they have as good a time as you. It is about intimacy, pleasure and finding new ways of sharing an extraordinary time with your partner. It is ensuring when your partner thinks about sex with you, they get a particular smile on their face, not a look of disappointment and wishful thinking when you have finished after 30 seconds and haven't thought about their pleasure at all.

The number of comments, threads and posts in the world talking about boyfriends or partners who don't engage in foreplay and then finish in no time flat, leaving their partners unsatisfied and fed up is pretty phenomenal. These posts sit alongside conversations with female friends and colleagues over the years where the same story is repeated again and again. The guys they are with just don't care about them, about their pleasure, about finding out how to touch them, about anything but their own satisfaction.

The losses for guys who engage in this very self-involved kind of attitude are significant. These losses might not be felt immediately, but they will come to impact you later, when one day you actually have mind and body altering sex because you actually cared about your partner and you realise what you have been missing all this time.

And these losses take a couple of different shapes. The first is one where you eventually realise you were quite selfish and your self-obsession meant you dismissed your partner's needs almost as soon as you got excited and after finishing quickly you didn't think to ensure she was having a good time. The realisation is you experienced around 2% of what might have been possible in those circumstances. And the understanding of what might have been possible in those circumstances will play on your mind.

The second aspect of these losses is you will get a reputation for being inconsiderate in bed and being someone who doesn't care about who he is with. No-one wants to lie there feeling used and abused for someone else's sexual satisfaction, having chosen to share their body and vulnerability with this person.

Pretty soon, it doesn't matter how good looking you are, or how successful you are, you will get a reputation for being self-absorbed in potentially intimate scenarios. Once you get a reputation it sticks and there is almost nothing you can do to fix it.

The opposite is also true, in that you can build the confidence to be a considerate, skilled and awesome partner. When this happens, you will be surprised to find there will be impact on not only the numbers of potential partners who make themselves available to you, but more importantly you will gain the respect of women who understand that you legitimately and truthfully take the time to pleasure your partners, meaning you are not selfish and you have a real and truthful respect for women. This is gold, and ultimately what this book is about.

But physically guys this book is aimed at supporting you to be amazing in bed with whomever you choose to have sex with. For clarity and transparency this is a book with a focus on males having sex with females. Guys if you are interested in having sex with other guys, then you will need to read a different book.

While this book is about sex, it is also about Respect and Pleasure.

The premise of this book is to teach you how to have great sex, but it is also about getting you to change your focus about sex away from yourself and toward the pleasure of your partner.

If you approach sex from the view of having great respect for women, for their bodies, their choices, their Pleasure, their everything, the sex you will have will be mindbogglingly extraordinary. Conversely if you have no respect for women, have no respect for their bodies, their choices, their Pleasure and their everything and you will have boring, poor and bad sex, and you might find yourself making choices about consent and power you will regret for the rest of your life. If you aren't sure what is meant by consent and power, keep reading.

This isn't a scare tactic, a shaming exercise or a desire to inhibit your choices in the future. This is an opportunity for you to open your eyes, potentially change the course of your thinking and your actions and make some amazing choices as the adventure of your life really takes off.

Something this book isn't is a lecture. This isn't a lecture on what you should and shouldn't be doing. Those options are written about here but take of them what you will. The simple fact is I wish I had this book to read when exploring sex for the first time and then for the subsequent couple of years when I was working it all out. Would have helped me enormously. The Joy of Sex just didn't cut it. Drawings of people who look like your parents having sex isn't exactly inspiring. You could say I have written this retrospectively for myself. And here it is for you.

8

Your Parents

You probably don't want to think about the relevant adults in your life having sex. But they did. And they probably still do.

One of the challenges you might be facing at the moment is going to be your relationship with your parents, how they are talking to you or not talking to you about sex, and their potentially complex relationship with sex.

They are likely to be completely confused by how to talk to you about sex.

You are the first generation in history to grow up with access to 24hr porn. Which means they are the first generation of parents in history to have to work out how to be parents to young people who have had 24hr access to porn.

Added to this are the challenges of their relationship to sex, their own experience of being your age and exploring sex for the first time, the relationships they had with their own parents and a whole range of other things.

You might not know, but the vast majority of your parents

won't have seen porn or anything like porn when they were your age. Their first experiences of sex will probably have been with someone else who didn't know what they were doing either. They will both have been fumbling about and hoping to get it right. They didn't have the pressures you all have due to porn and social media.

Parenting your children as they go through various stages of puberty and adolescence often means reflecting on your own experiences of that time as some measure of how you are going to help your children through it, or not as some will choose to do.

Your parents have no experience of what you are going through. But what they will have is a desire for you to be safe and to have consensual experiences at all times. And if you are having sex, they will probably be wanting you to enjoy the experience rather than have bad experiences. They might not say this, but there are very few parents out there who want their children to have bad sex.

Try to have conversations with them about sex. Ask them questions. It might be up to you to start these conversations if they aren't going to. This is similar to the chapter about talking to your potential partners about sex and that it is seen as a 'difficult' conversation. The more you talk to your parents about sex the easier it gets.

And be gentle with them and be kind if they seem out of touch. They are going through the serious challenge of parenting you at this time. It isn't easy.

9

The challenges of being a young man exploring sex for the first couple of years.

There are a couple of elements here.

1. You as a young man are expected to know what you are doing when you are having sex. And how can you know if you have no experience?
2. You have been brought up in a world discriminating against women. To have extraordinary sex, you need to push back against this.
3. Your experience of sex has in all likelihood been defined by porn, and this is the poorest teacher of sex you could find. This isn't your fault.

This last point is extraordinarily important.

This isn't your fault and it is very important you don't feel any shame about this. There is no other information available to you that can help you. Conversations about sex are framed in such a way so people find them intensely difficult to have, with the result being no one has them. So there is no shame in having porn as your teacher. But as you will see by reading on, there are other ways to your sexual future, and other choices to make in terms of your sexual life.

In your journey into intimacy and sex there are a range of challenges facing you, both obvious and systemic to our culture, but there are also lots of things you can do to have an extraordinary time.

You will have spent the entirety of your life so far surrounded by a world consciously and subconsciously telling you women are inferior to men. This will have happened from before you can remember, to something happening yesterday you may or may not have been aware of.

You will have seen these things in front of your own eyes, specific put-downs to girls at school or outside school, from either teachers or fellow pupils, for which those on the receiving end probably had no answer, as it is not something anyone is naturally equipped to tackle.

It isn't just a school issue either. This degrading, putting down, diminishing and dehumanising of women happens across our culture.

Our culture is full of films, TV, and games dominated by men, usually white, and with very few women in leading roles or with the same kind of power or authority represented by men. Look at these things through the lens of the Bechdel test and see if any pass. (The Bechdel test is a measure of representation of women in media. With regard to film it asks whether two women in a movie talk about something other than a man)

And you may well have been around when blokes were putting women down, and maybe you challenged the arguments and maybe, like the majority of men, you didn't.

Added to this will be, and this is where porn comes in, the pursuit of a woman's pleasure and ecstasy just doesn't happen. This is where the majority of the cultural experiences we have representing or showing intimacy and sex are geared toward ensuring the men involved are pleasured by women and his pleasure is primary and hers is secondary, if it is even shown at all. This isn't all cultural representations of intimacy and pleasure, but it is going to be the most you will see.

So with this background and history you have your work cut out for you. You have to consciously challenge these assumptions in all aspects of your life. You have to push back against the guys who say women are inferior. The reality is these guys are terrified of acknowledging how extraordinary women are. They are terrified that the narratives about women they have had drummed into them all their lives are wrong. But it is these narratives that are wrong. Terribly, terribly wrong..

There are a number of significant impacts a lack of respect for women has on women. Writing them all here would create another book, so I'm not going to give an exhaustive list, but a short one will include - rape, domestic violence, domestic killing, slut shaming, revenge porn, online trolling, online bullying, inequality in pay, inequality in rights, the assumption that the state has a say over the choices a woman makes with her body, fear of walking down the street, during daylight and at night, running by themselves..... The list is unfortunately endless because this is our world.

The area we are talking about in this book is sex. Specifically what I have written about here is a guide to sex for the inexperienced, and experienced as well, because lets face it, just because you are experienced doesn't make you good. You could be experienced in all the wrong ways. This book is a way through which deep, deep respect and love of women can manifest and as a result glorious and incredible experiences can be had by all. It is also a guide to pleasure, to finding the pleasure in exploring the wonders of the women you are with and having a very sexy, very intimate time with them. If enough young men, and women, read this book, implement the exercises and take time to explore sex and respect with each other, we will make a better world.

Because great sex whenever you have sex is available to all.

10

You are supposed to be good in bed even though you have no experience.

Another reality you have to engage with is that you are expected to know what to do and how to be amazing in bed from the get-go. Who is expected to be brilliant at something they have never done before? Yet this is the expectation we have all experienced. And while there might not be anyone who says this explicitly to you, this pressure, this expectation is in the world and will also be in your head.

I suspect this is some of the reason for a lot of young guys treating women so badly during sex. They are so intimidated by the expectation to be amazing in bed they turn it around by being self-centred and bully her into doing whatever they want, turning the situation into one where there is no expectation on him to show any interest or intimacy. You can really only get better at being incredible in bed by having sex and having sex with someone who is interested in working with you to make it extraordinary. This book is not a replacement for experience. This book is a guide to help you when you get there, to give you answers to questions you didn't even know you had yet, and to give you a framework to work off.

11

Are you willing to learn, change and grow?

Before we get into the details, the biggest question you need to ask yourself is: Are you willing to learn, to change and to grow?

A lot of what is to come in this book is the opposite of what you might have learnt from watching porn. There are a range of different behaviours I am suggesting you engage with. Some of these are going to be the opposite of what you might currently believe to be how you should behave when in an intimate encounter.

So are you willing to learn and to change and therefore to grow? You might be reading this and thinking everything in the book describes you anyway. Great, but even if this is the case, you still have to be willing to learn and to grow as you gain more experience and knowledge. Sometimes change can be really tough to deal with. You can do it. Your sexual future awaits.

12

Masculinity. What makes you a man?

A challenge you are likely to come up against when focusing on the pleasure of your partner is the idea that doing so makes you somehow less of a 'man' or less 'masculine' and that a 'real man' wouldn't waste their time on thinking about their partner because being a real man means your priorities are number one and everyone else is irrelevant.

We are told, primarily by TV and Film worlds, that being a man means not crying, being able to beat everyone up, not caring about others or about your partner, dealing with pain without showing it and the one that is most relevant to us, using sex as some sort of demonstration of power and dominance.

This couldn't be further from the truth.

Being a 'real man' means caring about others, especially your partner, being engaged with your emotions and, with most relevance to us, having a shared intimate experience with your partner where conversation and connection happens through an exploration of her pleasure.

There is a new term you might have heard of, and there are bound to be many more. The term is 'Simp' and is a negative term for someone who shows excessive sympathy or attention toward someone else, usually female. Another definition is someone who is overly submissive toward a female or their partner. So being interested in someone else's feelings and affections is a negative. This is ridiculous.

I think the reality here is that those using these terms are jealous. Jealous of the amazing time the 'simp' is having with their girlfriend. Jealous of what they might perceive as the courage of that guy to be emotionally available to his girlfriend. Jealous of the amazing intimate times he is having.

There is a book to be written about the realities of being a real man vs the images pushed at us day and night. The main reality you need to understand is that being emotionally and physically engaged with your partner and focusing on her pleasure when you are having an intimate encounter is the centre of all of it. And if people call you Simp for doing so, then best ignore them and spend time with people who understand.

13

There are two rules: Consent and Safety

The first thing you have to know about sex is that there are two rules. Most of what you will read about in the rest of this book is essentially about these two rules.

The first is Consent. There has to be consent from both sides. Consent from your partner. Consent from you.

The second rule is safety. You both have to be safe and feel safe. Safe means a range of things. Safe in terms of STI's, emotionally safe, physically safe, socially safe.

Further on in the book I will talk about things that might seem a bit weird, a bit of a kink or a bit taboo. Everything is possible in your sexual relationships, as long as there is consent and both parties are safe.

Consensual and Safe. The 2 rules.

14

If you are going to have sex with your girlfriend, do it properly (where sex education has failed)

Sex education in schools is a very important element of education, but the challenge is it isn't done properly. Most sex education is about safe sex, consensual sex, don't get pregnant sex and, a lot of the time, don't have sex sex. This is all super important information and very necessary for the education of young people. Considering the politics and social dynamics of our world at the minute, drumming into boys the reality of No means No, not maybe in a minute or I really mean yes, but No, is unbelievably important.

What is missing is how to have amazing sex. This isn't telling 13 and 14 year olds they need to have as much sex as they can with each other, but rather it is saying, despite the restrictive christian morality still surrounding sex and sex in education, sex is something that needs to be explored, needs to be with someone you want to be with and you need to take time to get to grips with how your body responds to certain actions and attentions.

What is missing for boys is a detailed understanding of how to pleasure a partner. None of us ever learned this. Growing up there was no access to information as to how we were going to be a considerate and successful partner.

The information needed is also one about taking time to explore yourself, alongside taking time to explore your partner.

15

If you want to have incredible sex with someone, you are going to have to learn to talk about it

One of the reasons why everyone has abandoned you all when it comes to sex is that the people who should be talking to you about it don't know how to talk about it themselves. Having difficult conversations is something that is avoided by most people, most of the time. These conversations might not be difficult ones, they are just assumed to be difficult because everyone says they are. Sometimes they aren't difficult either, they are just uncomfortable.

You will quickly find that once you start, what you thought would be difficult conversations quickly reveal themselves not to be difficult. Often we find ourselves talking about things we hadn't ever shared with anyone, and we finish these 'difficult' conversations feeling very different about ourselves and those we have spoken to.

This is the reality with talking about sex with your partner or potential partner. You might have read this chapter header about talking about sex and thought 'not on your life' / 'not going to happen'. You might squirm and feel incredibly uncomfortable about talking about it, and your partner might squirm and feel uncomfortable about it. But when you begin, and you just have to start, you will soon realise it is much easier than you thought.

The first sentences might feel weird. It might make you want to run away because you feel embarrassed. This is OK. But you need to keep going. Keep talking. Remember that your partner is probably feeling the same way, so the best way to make her feel better and stronger about talking is to really listen to what she is saying. It is the same as if you are with her in an intimate encounter. Focus on her.

These conversations could be about what you both like, what you don't, what you want to explore that you haven't explored, your histories, anything about sex. What you will find is that once you have had that first conversation, then the next time you talk about sex it will be easier, then the next time even easier, until talking about sex just becomes normal.

Then if you start having sex with someone else, the fact that you are so comfortable talking about it will be a big bonus. What you will also find is that 'difficult' conversations about other topics will become easier to have. So if you get comfortable talking about sex, then you will probably be comfortable talking about a whole range of taboo subjects, or subjects that previously you will have avoided.

If you do start talking about sex with a new partner, be aware that they may not have had the experience you have had, so go gently to begin with. They will quickly get used to it.

16

In these conversations the listening is more important than the talking.

In the conversations you are going to have with your partner, whether about sex or about any other subject, your listening is more important than your talking.

When was the last time you actually listened to what your partner was saying to you? This might not be about sex, this might be about something completely different. Do you truly listen? Or when they talk is your mind somewhere else? Maybe you are wanting to jump in with another thought of your own? Maybe you try to finish her sentence?

Don't do this. Listen. Actively listen to what they are saying. Ask them questions about what they are saying so you truly understand it. Extraordinary things happen when you actively listen to someone and give them the space to speak and to talk about what is important to them. What they talk about changes. They share incredible things with you.

Have you ever been in a situation where you are talking to someone who isn't really interested in talking to you? You just stop sharing anything interesting with them. You get the sense of 'You don't care about this conversation so I'm not going to give you anything of me'. The opposite happens when you truly listen. People share themselves with you because they are being heard.

So shut up and listen and listen with all of your attention. You will be amazed at what happens both to what your partner is saying but also to your relationship.

17

Sex isn't finished when you are finished. Sex is a journey not a destination

I think this is a major reason guys, and especially girls, are having bad sex.

There is a general idea for blokes that when they have finished, which is defined by ejaculation, then that is the end of the sexual encounter. This is perpetuated by porn, where the whole scene is always moving toward the money shot, and when this has happened, the sex is finished. This is generally the story with a significant amount of sex in partnerships and can be deeply frustrating for the female, as the guy is generally done just as she is getting into it. Without understanding intimacy, without understanding the reality of how to support their partner's pleasure, it happens time and time again. This then happens so frequently the female in the partnership no longer has much interest in sex with their boyfriend/partner as they know they won't be satisfied in any way.

This is not the reality of how you should be thinking about sex with your girlfriend or partner. Just because you have finished, doesn't mean she has. Sometimes when you are having a fantastic time with your girlfriend you might just find you finish sooner than you wanted or expected to. For some this can be quite a problem, but for most of us, this might be because we haven't had sex for a while, are particularly sensitive during the session….. There are a range of reasons.

But the reality is, just because you have finished doesn't mean the sex you are having is over. It might be, your partner might be mightily satisfied with what has gone on. But often they haven't had their full possibility of pleasure.

So how about you rethink this?

How about you change your thinking and action to think the sex you are having isn't finished until your partner is finished, and then think about what this means. Is it finished for her if defined as 1 orgasm? Is it 3? Is it 10? Maybe there isn't an orgasm, instead she wants to experience a sustained feeling of deep pleasure from the tips of her toes to the top of her head.

So when you have finished, rather than falling asleep or doing whatever you might do, turn your attention to her. Get your hands and fingers back involved, your mouth involved. Slow down, speed up, whatever, but focus on getting your partner flying. You might also find that by doing so gets you hard again, so you can continue as well.

By doing this, and regularly continuing after you have finished, your sex life will be incredible and your partner will know you are properly focused on her, and you aren't just there for your own gratification.

Don't be one of those guys who shoots and finishes.

On the opposite end of this experience, if you know you are likely to ejaculate quite quickly, being super sensitive and ready to go at any second, then ensure you prolong even further the foreplay you are exploring. We talk a lot about foreplay and it is incredibly important you truly engage in foreplay with your partner as, from a woman's perspective, it can be disheartening if a partner doesn't seek foreplay first before thinking about getting his end away. This kind of thinking is why this book exists.

So if you think you are likely to finish quickly, take longer in foreplay. Then when you have finished, get back involved.

There is a strong possibility the first time you continue the pleasure after you have finished will really surprise and delight her and the fun you will have together will be amazing.

18

Foreplay is Sex

Foreplay isn't something that happens before you get to the sex you are wanting to have. Foreplay is part of the sex you are having.

Remember, we are focusing on sex as a journey encompassing everything you experience in an intimate encounter, rather than a physical action driving to a destination, your ejaculation. With the focus on everything you do on the journey as a part of sex, exploring foreplay is part of having sex with your partner.

Foreplay is probably the most important thing for you to understand when you are focusing on your partner and how they can have an incredible time.

The more time you spend on foreplay and on making her feel incredible, the better time you will both have. Sometimes this isn't the case, where she might be feeling like she wants to jump straight into having you inside her, or you might only have a short amount of time together. Generally though, the more time you spend with foreplay, the better time you will both have.

19

Foreplay isn't only what you do when you are beginning your sexual adventure

While foreplay is mostly discussed as the 'warming up' actions you are both involved in before you generally get to penetration, this isn't the only definition. There is another element of foreplay that you should think about in much more detail and that is what happens in the hours before you get to take each others' clothes off.

For example, let's say you are anticipating a hot and sexy evening together. The foreplay I am talking about here really starts when you are first together. It might be the morning, early afternoon, or even early evening. When you see her for the first time on that day how do you greet her? How you look at her is foreplay. How you touch her is foreplay. How you kiss her is foreplay. It might be 12 hours until you get your clothes off, but this layering of the anticipation, the touch, the excitement, will have significant impact on what happens later.

Throughout the time you are together how do you touch her? When you are holding her hand are you really feeling the contact of your skin, the pressure of your palms together, the feeling of what that touch is like? Or are you limply holding her hand because she wants you to? Your active presence and choices in how you do these things throughout your time together impact what happens later.

A word of warning though. Don't be over the top about it or get creepy with it. There are sexy, exciting ways to keep your touch, eye contact and anticipation of pleasure positive and not over the top, then there are the ways of overdoing it that mean you will just come across as creepy. Don't be creepy.

Keep these things small and not obvious. It might be that she doesn't even notice them. If she doesn't notice them, like a touch on an arm or how you hold her hand, don't tell her about it. She will notice eventually. It is better to do less than to do more.

Ultimately, remember that foreplay isn't just for your bedroom. Foreplay can last all day.

20

Self Pleasure –Exploring yourself. Knowing yourself. Can we stop thinking wanking is a bad thing please!! You have permission to explore your own pleasure without shame.

With the central idea of this book being about focusing on your partner's pleasure when you are being intimate, we also need to talk about self pleasure. Exploring yourself and your own pleasure still seems to get a bad rap and where the idea of a male exploring his own pleasure is considered to be wrong or taboo. The consequence of this is male self pleasure then becomes shameful and it becomes something you do secretly in the dark.

What we have also come to is self pleasure only really happens when viewing porn, so the reality here is time spent actually exploring what feels good and focusing on the multitude of sensations you can experience in your body doesn't really happen because the porn makes you accelerate toward ejaculation, and as quickly as possible because it is still presented as a shameful act. This means you are focused on the end of your cock, not on how the rest of you is feeling or responding to what is going on.

Spend time without porn and without external stimulus while pleasuring yourself. If you haven't done this for awhile or ever, maybe you start your pleasure session like this then finish with what you currently do. Build yourself to a position of having self pleasure sessions without porn on a regular basis, maybe once a week, maybe twice a week.

What you will find is the physical sensations you experience will increase the more you focus on them. You will begin to understand how different touch gives different sensations, how different speed, amounts of friction, all these things we are exploring in this book to support women's pleasure, can augment your own pleasure.

You have permission to do this. This is not a shameful act. The idea of self pleasure as a bad thing is linked to old ideas of religion and spiritual cleanliness. Ignore this. You have permission to find out about yourself, to find what you like, what you don't and what you might want to explore with someone else.

In the spirit of reciprocity, and I talk a little about this with anal sex, explore the taste and texture of your own cum. Now some of you might have read this and you can't quite believe it has been suggested, but there is a general expectation that if your sexual partner is going to go down on you they will have cum in their mouth. You might not finish in their mouth, but it is likely some pre-cum will find its way there. Some of you might also expect your partner will swallow when you cum in their mouth. This is an interesting expectation and one that isn't often challenged. If you expect them to fill their mouth with your cum, shouldn't you at least know what you are expecting them to taste?

If you don't have permission to explore your own pleasure, then how can you successfully focus on the pleasure of someone else? If you bring a sense of shame and embarrassment about your own pleasure explorations to an intimate experience with someone else, then you are going to be inhibited in supporting someone else's pleasure, and possibly in ways you don't even realise. Now, if you have friends who get this, then talk with them about it. You will probably have friends who do get it and will talk about it and others with whom there is no way you will discuss this.

Explore yourself. Play with yourself. Pleasure yourself.

21

Sex isn't penetration.

Sex isn't penetration. Penetration is a part of sex, but it isn't all of sex. In fact, if you are doing it by this book, it is a small percentage of sex. Sex is everything. It is touch, kissing, holding onto each other, getting your hands involved, getting your mouth involved, the minutes before you start, the minutes after you finish.

There are multiple aspects to what sex is, and penetration is just one of those aspects. It is an exquisitely fun aspect, but just one aspect. Don't get caught into thinking this is all sex is. If this is what you think, then unfortunately you are going to have a very limited experience of the amazing, intimate pleasures awaiting you.

Explore intimacy without penetration. What happens if you only use your hands? What happens if you only use your mouth? She might do the same with you. Not every intimate encounter needs to involve penetration.

Remember, the rules are simple. Consent and Safety. How you choose to explore sex within consent and safety is as varied as you choose to make it.

22

Males experience sex very differently to females. This is physiological reality.

The male experience of sex and arousal is very different to the female experience.

We blokes can get hard within seconds of having thoughts and feelings about sex, about someone, about most things. Most of us have experienced a spontaneous boner in public before. You are trying not to think of the very sexy image that has come into your mind, but, to no avail and, four seconds later, enormous boner in your trousers. Sometimes you don't even need this. Sit on a bus or train and the vibration can give you what was always called a 'travel fat'.

The reality then when we are having sex is that frequently we can be finished in minutes. So a very quick arousal and a quick finish. This isn't true of everyone, and some guys find it very hard to finish. But these are relatively rare exceptions.

For women this is different. This is a generalisation, and

not all women would agree, but it generally takes longer for women to be aroused, certainly to the level of thundering boner taking us all of four seconds to get. For a lot of women this could take minutes. And the reality here is if you rush into things, her arousal may never happen.

(There is an interesting theory about sex you might find useful, called the Dual Control Theory, and this is essentially excitement (accelerator) and inhibition (brake). In a very simplistic way, the accelerator of excitement and the brake of inhibition are the two extremes we are balancing in all aspects of our sexual lives, from the anticipation to being in the throws of sexual exploration, whether solo or with a partner, and your partner is going to be going through as well. The more you are aware of these working in yourself, the more you will be aware of them working in your partner and the more you are going to be able to have greater understanding of consequences of what you do)

Then when we are in the midst of sex, often it will take longer for women to reach orgasm than us. Their pay off here is they can often then have multiple orgasms, so the time taken to get there is paid off with continuous and mind-warping orgasms. We are also able to have multiple orgasms, it just takes practice. It is important you know this difference. Remember, these are generalisations.

Sometimes it might take you a couple of minutes to get fully hard. Sometimes it just takes longer. And sometimes you might last for an hour without finishing. Sometimes you might not finish. This is OK. You don't always need to finish.

Remember there are no formal rules you need to follow for how to have sex, except the rules of Consent and Safety. Everything is an experiment in maximising intimacy and pleasure.

23

The anti-pornification of intimacy. Your girlfriend is not your own personal porn star. Unless she wants to be...

So porn is everywhere. In fact porn is far and away the most consumed content on the internet. And the list of what can be watched is massive. Who is most of this porn made for? Blokes. And what is the intent of this porn? To take your money by getting you to sign up to websites and then to get you knocking one out within a couple of minutes. Set up the scene, get your cock out, the scene lasts for 10 minutes and you should have sorted yourself out by then.

These porn clips are giving you false information in a multitude of ways. 10 minutes is the average length of the majority of these clips. This is essentially telling you a sexual encounter, where 'all' parties are supposedly satisfied, will last this long. 2 minutes setting the scene, 2 minutes foreplay with 98% of this time involving the women sucking off the blokes, and around 5 ½ minutes of sex in various positions before he finishes on her face.

Most of these scenes also involve the men dominating the action, moving the women to wherever he wants them and where his desires come before hers, or theirs. At this point, there is often quite a lot of violence going on in these scenes. This involves a lot of slapping, mostly of arses, sometimes legs, sometimes breasts and sometimes faces. It often involves strangling, hair pulling and generally violent and demeaning action. This kind of violence doesn't always happen. Some porn films are gentle and careful and all participants look like they are enjoying themselves.

And this is the last bit of false information. Everyone looks like they are enjoying themselves. While sometimes they might be, oftentimes they are not.

Let's go back to the beginning. The 10 minute time frame. (Obviously there are much longer porn films, but what is being discussed here is the length of time of the porn clips on free to watch porn sites.)

Sometimes a quickie might be 10 minutes or less, but you should be thinking of this as the exception rather than the rule. 10 minutes should be the time it takes for you to begin getting your hands involved. 10 minutes should be the time you take to bring your girlfriend to her first orgasm with what you do with your hands. Another 10 minutes or so of going down on her followed by however long you want to get into sex in whatever positions you might want to play with. Minimum of 30 to 40 minutes, taking your time. Then when you have recovered, you can start again. This isn't a strict process or time frame, these elements are interchangeable, and need to be if you want to keep playing with new ideas.

I understand for some of you parents could be home any

minute, you just want to get it on. And sometimes the pressure of getting discovered can be quite exciting. I'm not talking about this. I'm talking about you having time to play and discover. 10 minutes isn't OK.

Next point. The men dominate the action. How about you get your girlfriend to tell you what she wants, to put herself where she wants to be and you facilitate this? How good would your sex be if she was to let you know exactly where and how she wants to be engaged with, the positions she wants to try and explore, and then you take it as your mission to find the ways through which you can ensure she hits the heights of ecstasy every time. There will be times when she wants you to dominate the action, to dictate what happens and how, but those decisions are made consensually. It isn't a given you are going to take control.

I'm not sure at what point it was decided smacking your girlfriend around while having sex with her was something exciting or desired. There is a reality that sometimes pain, mostly from pinching or a little bit more friction on the skin when stroking, and for others hot wax, when applied at the right time can bring desired responses. I go into a little of this further into the book with a chapter about touch. But smacking your girlfriend around the face? Or the one I truly don't understand, actually slapping all the sensitive areas needing to be properly stroked and cared for? This is the opposite of intimacy.

If your girlfriend is interested in these actions being done to her while in the middle of sex, then you need to ensure you have a 'safe' word she uses when she has had enough. But I would suggest the percentage of women in the world who want to be beaten up while involving themselves in a sexual encounter with their boyfriend is very, very low. Don't make the assumption she wants it just because you have seen it in a porn film. Much more likely if she has taken part in such activity in the past it is because she has been coerced into it by a partner who thought it was OK and she didn't feel strong enough or was too scared to say no. It may also be your partner has never had the experience where sex has been pleasurable, and has only had the experience of being 'done to' while having sex.

And lastly, the idea everyone in these porn films is having a good time. They're not. Sometimes they are, but remember they are paid 'actors' who are required to be having a super hot, super sexy time. This is not real. And this is not the real world. They aren't that wet. They use industrial amounts of lube.

With all of this said, there are some porn films and clips out there that are sexy, sensual, women dominating and well shot with performers having a very good time with each other. But I think these are the exceptions to the rule.

The point of this is to make it clear to you what you see in porn is not realistic, and therefore expecting your girlfriend to 'perform' for you as a porn star might, is not respectful, not realistic and not OK. If your girlfriend wants to 'perform' for you and be your own personal porn star then that is her choice and something she consents to, not a role she should be doing because it is what you expect from her.

If you follow my instructions below and get into your stride with what you can do together, you won't be needing porn anymore.

24

Final Bit about Porn. You need it harder and harder to get off, and it is going to lead you down some seriously dark rabbit holes you should be careful about exploring.

One of the other elements of porn you might have found for yourself is the more you use it to get yourself off, the more intense or the harder the sex you are watching will be.

Within quite a short amount of time the algorithms on these porn sites will start sending you porn that will be very intense and the more you watch, the more intense it will get.

There are two main consequences of this. The first is the intensity of the contact you are making with your cock when getting off is going to increase, because the more you get yourself off the less responsive the nerve endings so you then need to stimulate yourself harder. Not only are you numbing your cock, you are also going to be numbing yourself to some of the actions you are watching. The film where women are being slapped around, where there is general violence toward women, isn't going to elicit a feeling of worry for the women involved. You will probably have gotten used to seeing this kind of violence in this context and it will have become normalised. This then translates into the bedroom, where the idea of slapping your partner around, where previously you would have be horrified to do that, now seems normal.

The second thing is that the more you watch the more the algorithms will offer scenes not only containing increased levels of violence but also increasingly younger performers. A lot of porn you see online involves extremely young women, a significant number who are under age, and often coerced into performing. So you will be being directed to watch violence with underage performers who are under duress.

The situation then potentially becomes this. When you are then intimate with someone, you begin to replicate the porn you have been watching, because you think this is 'normal'. This might involve slapping your partner around, finishing on her face, strangling etc.… And your partner is most likely to be very surprised, challenged and traumatised by suddenly being assaulted when she thought you were having an intimate experience.

Finally, the age of the women you are watching may put you in a legally difficult situation where you are watching child porn, under the age of consent, without realising it. Not realising it isn't a good legal defense. Are you prepared for the consequences of doing this? So with all of these chapters on porn, I'm not trying to shame you into stopping watching it. You just have to be careful about and aware of what you watch.

25

What are you doing when you are being intimate with someone?

When I talk about being intimate with someone I am talking about a range of things. For the purpose of this book I will focus on a couple of definitions. Words you might associate with Intimacy might be: Sharing, touching, vulnerable, closeness, affection, tender, fragile, listening, reveal, trust, honesty, courage, care, being seen, cautious

Intimacy is the action of sharing yourself with someone else, or of someone sharing themselves with you. This action could be physical, could be emotional, could be spiritual. My focus on intimacy lies in the process of making yourself vulnerable to someone, and by doing so sharing with them a part of you not normally shared with most people.

This idea of vulnerability is an interesting one for males. We have been brought up to be told being vulnerable is not a masculine trait and showing vulnerability gives people an opening through which they can get you, leaving you open to attack as you are sharing information about yourself which, in the wrong hands, could be used badly. This is part of the same narrative telling us women are inferior to men because they are more 'emotional'. This is part of the nonsense of the 'boys don't cry' we get told at primary school. There are countless examples.

You have to fight this.

You have to fight this and find ways to vulnerability because it is through intimacy we experience profound moments in our sexual and relational lives. And yes, it might be that someone you shared deeply intimate sexual moments with might decide they don't want to be with you anymore.

Then sometimes the person you were so intimate with may use those intimate moments against you to make themselves less hurt by the break up. This could be in a verbal way in talking about your experiences negatively either to you or to friends and it could be flat out denial there was anything of intimacy involved in your moments together. There are many different ways this can happen. And the reality is it is probably inevitable this will happen at some point.

A lot of people decide the fear of someone using their vulnerability against them in this way is too much for them and they then choose to live a life of no moments of vulnerability to ensure emotional safety.

This is understandable but I would like you to think about the opposite being true. If you accept at some point you are probably going to get your heart broken, and it is going to be emotionally tough going for a short while, you will put yourself in a position where the incredible experience of sharing intimacy far outweighs the fear of someone being mean to you. The other option is a life of not experiencing all that is on offer to you.

The act of sex is in itself an intimate act, in a range of ways. You will mostly be getting naked in front of someone else. When this happens for the first couple of times and with each different partner it is a deeply vulnerable moment. What if they don't like the look of me naked? What if I don't like the look of them naked? What if they laugh at me? What if I laugh at them? What if she thinks my cock is too small? What if she thinks it is too big?

Then getting your hands involved with intimate parts you haven't ever involved yourself with. Here there is a massive vulnerability in both receiving and giving. What if she thinks I am fumbling around and I don't know what I am doing? And for her, receiving your touch is a deeply intimate and vulnerable act. What if he doesn't like the way I feel? What if I don't like what he is doing? Can I say? What happens if I ask him to stop? What if I really like what he is doing and he makes me orgasm? What is it like to orgasm in front of him? Super vulnerable moment. And on and on it goes.

The more you are 'into' each other, the more you trust each other and therefore the more you are able to relax into each other's physical and emotional embrace, the moment and the experience, the more vulnerable you become. You are sharing moments with someone and pursuing physical and emotional feelings that are potentially mind and body blowing, and it is through the sharing of these moments we truly connect to others.

The opposite of this is essentially a one-dimensional sex life meaning you 'get it done as quickly as possible'. As little true pleasure for either of you and ending in you shooting your load and being done. No journey, no mind and body blown and ultimately cold, robotic sex.

Finding intimacy in your sexual partnerships is the goal we are looking to achieve and what this book is all about, and what you will find is the journey getting there will be amazing, sometimes frustrating and sometimes heart breaking, but ultimately when you arrive the sex you share with others will be out of this world.

26

Consent

27

Consent - the reality is simple

Consent is a very simple thing. Is your potential partner saying no to sex? No consent. Is she asking you to stop? No consent. No consent. Is she potentially so inebriated or off her head on whatever she has taken she can't truly make a decision about anything? No Consent. Is there any indication, body language, facial expression, words or any other way of seeing she isn't enjoying herself? Is she giving you negative feelings about the experience you are having? Then you pause and see what is going on. And if she wants to stop, you stop.

Simple.

You might both be completely up for an encounter when you start, but she might lose the desire to continue right in the middle of everything. What do you do?

You stop.

Just because you are in the middle of everything doesn't mean you have a right to finish it. If she wants you to stop, you stop. You might be about to experience the greatest orgasm of your life. She says stop. You stop. You can sort yourself out later.

You may have read about guys who have been accused of sexual assault where there was consent at the beginning but she changed her mind during the encounter and the guys say they didn't realise she wanted to stop. They say they didn't see a change in body language, couldn't read her change in desire, couldn't hear her say stop. I think this is nonsense.

If you are in the middle of a sexual encounter with someone and she changes her mind, you will know about it. Her body language will change. Her responses to your touches and your actions will change. The way she is breathing will change. I don't believe these things won't be noticed by you. You can pretend not to notice, or pretend to be so inebriated you didn't notice, but the reality is you will know the truth of the encounter.

The consumption of alcohol and/or drugs seems to alter the idea of consent for some males. Consumption of drugs or alcohol of any kind means you should be on a heightened alert. We know alcohol and drug consumption takes away public and private inhibitions. Just because someone is less inhibited than their sober state doesn't mean what they say is any less real. One of the myths of rape, and believed by a lot of people, is rape is caused by alcohol. Rape isn't caused by alcohol. Rape is sex without consent.

Do guys really think if someone is so inebriated or high they are mostly unconscious, and therefore not physically able to say no, they are therefore saying yes? If your potential partner is so out of it she can't speak, let alone make a decision, then the assumption you must make is there is no consent. This means a BIG NO to having sex with her. If she can't say yes, then that is a no. Really simple.

This comes back to respect. You respect the person you are with to make a decision based on what they want, and if they aren't in a state to do so, then you don't ask her to make a decision. You make the decision and the decision is sex isn't happening. If you truly thought it was going to happen, then it will happen at another time, just not then and there.

The rise of the use of date rape drugs and the spiking of drinks also increases the fear for women around consent, around waking up during the middle of being raped and unable to do anything about it because they can't move due to the drugs in their system, or coming to consciousness and realising something horrendous has happened. These women are then subject to an enormous amount of shame: by the perpetrators, by the process they have to go through when going to the police, the invasive sampling, and then the still appalling attitudes of most of society who think it was her fault and she was responsible for leading these guys on and they weren't responsible for what they did.

Guys, you are responsible for changing this. You are responsible for standing up for all the women out there and pursuing Consent as a baseline for every encounter, especially when alcohol and drugs are involved.

Guys you are also responsible for challenging and then changing the attitudes of your friends and colleagues. If one of your male friends or colleagues has an attitude that does not fall in line with No means No, then you have to challenge it. You have to put him right. Someone will get hurt, and it will be part of their life forever. What he ultimately does won't be your responsibility, but you have to try.

Your friend will also do the 'I was drunk, I don't remember what happened.' You also have to call bullshit on this, both the words and attitude they must have to say this to you, but also the bullshit it is. Call bullshit on the whole thing.

There are many more males out there who respect and love women than there are males who will rape and take advantage of vulnerable women. The problem is we aren't making our voices heard. We need to. And if this friend refuses to budge, then drop him as a friend and make sure every female you know is aware of his attitude. Life is too short to spend time with guys who have no respect for women.

One of the common responses from guys who are challenged on this kind of attitude and this kind of behaviour is aggression, or an attitude they are 'only joking'. Both of these responses essentially demonstrate the fact you saying the way they are behaving is wrong is a massive challenge to their sense of self, and their sense of power and control in and of the world around them. If they are responding with aggression, don't back down. I'm not saying have a fight with them, but be strong, be solid in your position. They might grab a range of blokes who are like minded and target you. Grab a range of guys who are like minded and resist.

There are more of us than them, the challenge is they are generally louder and more aggressive than us, and they bully others into submission. This might take time, but we will win. And the only way we are going to be able to do so is by actively challenging these ideas and slowly but surely educating other men in what is right and what is not.

There is a crisis of sexual assault going on in our world. There is a feeling this is being caused by a significant population of men. I don't think it is. I think this is being led and caused by a very small population of men. But these men are the bullies and the aggressors, and other men let them get away with it because they don't want the confrontation, the potential fight, or the harassment that might come afterwards. We need to stand together and fight this. It might become aggressive. It might become violent. But we need to stand our ground and resist.

You also need to empower your female friends by making sure they understand you are with them, you are on their side and you support their right to live without the kind of fear rape engenders. You need to empower your family members, male and female, to ensure all males acknowledge this and all women feel strong enough to state their position when they need to.

Finally on consent, who wants to have sex with someone who doesn't want to? Someone who is doing it for a power trip and is so damaged with their own sense of self worth the only way they can satisfy it is to physically hold power over someone else.

Replace this with having extraordinary sex with someone who does want to. Replace it with the power experienced when you are sharing your vulnerability with someone.

This is power, this is the power of engaging with and embracing one of the most extraordinary experiences we can have as humans.

28

Non-consensual sex when in relationships.

All of the above also applies to you when you are in a relationship. Just because you are in a relationship with someone doesn't mean consent changes. It doesn't mean you 'own' them and you can have your way with them whenever you want to.

Does she want to have sex with you? No? Then it doesn't happen. No attempted coercing, physically or emotionally.

No means no. In or out of a relationship.

29

Consent also applies to you and your choices

Consent also applies to you. If someone is propositioning you for sex, you don't have to say yes. If you don't want to have sex with someone, then say no.

There is a large assumption about young men, that if someone so much as breathes on them they will want to have sex with them and if anyone wanted to have sex with them they would. This just isn't true.

You will find yourself in positions where someone wants to be intimate with you and for whatever reason, you don't want to be intimate with them. It could be you just don't fancy them, they are your friend, they are too forceful and a bit scary.....to be honest it doesn't matter the reason, the reason is irrelevant. If you don't want to have sex with someone, then say no.

And as with any situation where you will reject someone's advances, be friendly about it, be nice, be kind, be careful. When we are rejected the worst thing is to have someone then humiliate you with the way they reject you, so be careful you don't do this to others. We have all felt the uncomfortable feeling of rejection and if you are able to spare someone else that feeling, please try to.

This also holds true if you are in a relationship. If your partner is feeling amorous and you aren't, just say no.

Consent goes both ways.

30

Girls like sex too

31

Girls like sex too, but only consensual and when they are respected and treated properly

Girls like sex too.

For whatever reason, and this was never said explicitly to me or my friends by anyone in school or at home, I grew up with the idea that girls didn't like sex. That sex was something guys 'did' and girls kind of just dealt with it. I don't know why this was the case and I can't pinpoint a time when it came into my head, but it was probably the conservative culture of the time. The reality was it inhibited me in my actions in pursuing intimacy with girls because I felt if I made moves toward having sex with them they would think I was a dick for doing so and I would lose their friendship and respect.

There is something about this attitude that was helpful, so when I did have sex with someone, it had been built up to and we both really wanted to get it on. There wasn't ever a partner or moment that felt forced or where one of us didn't want to be there. So maybe this wasn't such a bad thing.

So the reality is girls like sex too. Just in case you didn't realise, girls want to be exploring themselves and you as much as you want to be exploring yourself and them, but the culture we are in doesn't allow this to be played out in the way it should.

Despite #metoo, despite all the articles and conversations in the media, the reality is there are barriers to this. And one of these barriers is young men are taught or are led to believe through media, their own hype and macho attitudes, their peers and sometimes families, they are the dominant gender and they can take and have sex with whomever they like.

Sometimes this isn't obvious and can be sly and manipulative. Sometimes and more often than I think most of us want to admit, the subconscious manipulation of young men into thinking they can do what they like means they don't actually understand their actions. They get a rod on and therefore they need to have sex with someone. They think this is a privilege girls need to afford them. This isn't excusing it. Just an observation.

Alongside this, girls are told by society, media and peer pressure to hide their sexuality, to hide their desire and their interest in sex. They are told very clearly if they enjoy sex and have lots of sex then they are a Slut, whereas if boys have lots of sex they are a Legend. This kind of disparity is ingrained in our world and is going to be a massive challenge to fix.

One of the ways we can fix it is to respect girl's desires to enjoy and explore sex and share with them the best time they can possibly have, while affording them all the space and time to say no whenever they wish to. And the other aspect of this, written about in more detail elsewhere, is if you have sex with someone, you keep the details of it to yourself.

So much slut-shaming and reputation destroying happens when guys decide they need to get some sort of status by talking about their conquests and the result is their partner gets absolutely slammed by it. Often the event is made out to be more than it was in order to create a greater impact on the story and therefore increase legend status of the bloke. And in addition, sometimes guys talk about having sex with someone they haven't had sex with. Just to build their sorry little ego. This kind of thing destroys people's lives.

As stated everywhere else in this writing, everything sexual has to be consensual. Added to this, it has to be with respect, dignity and care. This doesn't mean all the sex you have has to have soft lighting and whale music and candles. What it means is you are getting into it as one half of a unit of glorious sex, rather than as someone a girl sorts out. Where this happens could be in the middle of the day on a beach, late at night, in a car, in a forest, in your bedroom, you name it, day or night. It just has to have the care, respect and dignity for your partner the act of consensual sex requires.

32

Girls have also been sold a lie by porn

Similar to the way you have been sold a lie by porn, so too girls have been sold a lie. The lie you have all been sold is the idea that what you see in porn is real. More specifically, the lie to you is that sex is about you being 'serviced', about the power dynamic of sex being overly physical and aggressive toward your partner, and that when you are finished, the whole encounter is done.

The lie girls have been sold is the opposite of this. That their role in a sexual encounter is that they need to 'service' you, that they are submissive and need to passively accept whatever aggression and violence might happen to them while having sex, and that when you are finished, that is the end.

The central theme to this lie for girls is that no-one is interested in their pleasure and that pleasure in sex is only for guys. Some porn is the opposite of this, where there are specific categories showing female orgasm and others showing squirting, which is sometimes accompanied by orgasm but often not. The reality is that the vast majority of porn demonstrates a clear lack of interest in the pleasure of the female performer. You might see a female performer experiencing pleasure, but it isn't the focus of what you are watching and it is more than likely being faked.

Your role in exploring your sexual life and in focusing on the pleasure of your partner is to create the experience for your partner that is the opposite of what they have been brainwashed to believe. They aren't there to 'service' you. They are there as one in a partnership of adventures into pleasure. Your role is to create the most extraordinary and pleasurable experience with and for her.

They shouldn't expect aggression or violence from you at any point. Young women are talking across the internet about their experiences of choking and hair pulling becoming normal in sexual encounters. Don't do it guys. It is not normal and it is not OK. Your partner should not be fearing that you will be aggressive and violent toward her. (If your partner likes and consents to a more aggressive approach in an intimate encounter then you must have safe words to use if it gets too much.)

Finally, as it stated many times elsewhere in the book, when you are finished it doesn't mean she is. Keep going, get your hands and mouth back involved. This doesn't always have to happen, but it is important that you understand everything doesn't stop when you do.

You and your partner have been sold a lie by porn and it is important you understand the lie she has been sold as much as your own.

33

Intense, lose yourself sex

As briefly discussed above, there are lots of different places you can have sex and lots of different ways sex can impact you and your partner. This range of possibilities is quite something when it comes down to it.

A quickie when you are pushed for time, hours and hours of indulgent lust when you have the opportunity, different places, different environments both created by you and offered by the world, different positions, different amounts of effort and focus, different roles and altering leading and responding. Added to this is the difference between first thing in the morning, the middle of the day, late at night etc... makes what happens, what you do and the subsequent range of feelings it engenders in you such an amazing variety of possibilities.

The title of this little section is Intense, lose yourself Sex. What this describes is sexual encounters where the like and lust for and with your partner are heightened, your whole body is tingling, your skin nerve endings are firing in waves just from being present with someone you desperately want to get it on with. Making the barest of contact with this person is buzzing you, kissing them is amplifying this feeling up another 200%, full body contact with them does even more and you feel like you are going to absolutely explode with an indescribable feeling of lust and intensity of feeling.

Intense, lose yourself sex, where the whole world is reduced to you and your partner, and your feelings and explorations with your partner have led you to be in such a heightened awareness of each other and of yourselves.

Part of this heightened feeling might be having encounters in unusual places. Part of it might be you are about to get busted by people, parents, friends, siblings. But mostly these kinds of encounters happen when you are in a safe and undisturbed place, where you have all the time in the world to indulge in whatever explorations you want to involve yourself in.

One of the biggest challenges for you when you are indulging in this kind of Sex is to not get so overwhelmed by feelings and sensations you finish too early, but if you do, as stated earlier, you aren't finished. There are a couple of actions you can try to mitigate against this outcome. Sometimes you might just need to stop so your nerve endings pause in their frictioned sensation. This moment of stopping can actually be a very beautiful thing. Sometimes you don't need to stop but merely slow down, again to inhibit those nerve endings sending you over the edge.

The reality is the process of stopping yourself finishing too early can also be used to elongate the time and experience of the encounter for your partner, so rather than it being a moment of 'waiting for you to cool down', you use the time as an opportunity to focus on her while you step back from the edge of the precipice.

The reason for writing about Intense, lose yourself Sex is it is a perfect illustration of the experience you can have when you combine your overwhelming lust and desire for someone with the well of respect you have for them, their choices and their experiences and the mutual consent you have to indulge in epic and mind-blowing sex.

It is the perfect example of when Intimacy, and the opening of yourself to a vulnerable place when sharing yourself with someone, leads to experiences you won't ever forget.

34

The size of your cock really is irrelevant.

Let's talk about one of the elephants in the room when it comes to blokes and sex.

The size of your cock.

The reality of incredible sex is the size of your cock really is irrelevant. Short one, long one, thin, fat, bendy, straight. It doesn't matter. The sooner you accept this, the better.

Remember, penetration is one small aspect of sex. The size of your cock doesn't define whether you are good in bed or not. In fact, if you have an enormous cock then you might think you don't need to do anything else because your cock will magically make your partner orgasm every time you have sex, because this is what happens, right?

Actually, the reality of having a large cock is you need to go slow to begin with, and make sure you are using plenty of lube. Sometimes a large cock can hurt for both you and your partner if you don't go slowly to start.

Penetration doesn't make orgasms happen. Clitoral stimulation makes orgasms happen. Yes, sometimes orgasms happen with penetration, but mostly this is because the clitoris is still being stimulated in some way at the same time.

So in this scenario, you might be hung like a horse, but you won't bring much fun to exploring incredible sex. And also, sometimes an enormous cock just feels uncomfortable. Remember, just as we blokes are all different sizes, women have different sized vaginas and vulvas and clitoris'. Some of them are large, some small, some deep, some shallow, some with their clitoris close to the vaginal opening, some further away, some with the body of the clitoris shallow to the skin, some deeper. And sometimes an enormous cock just won't fit, or will be so uncomfortable sex has to stop.

We are all different and we are all unique. This is one of the great beauties of being human. None of us are the same.

Embrace what you have. Love what you have. Read this book multiple times to give yourself the skills to be incredible in bed, no matter the size of your cock

35

The size of your Bollocks is irrelevant

Alongside the size of your cock being irrelevant, so is the size of your bollocks. Guys, our testicles come in all sizes. Some have smaller testicles, some people have testicles they find challenging to fit into their underwear. Some have extra plumbing, so their scrotum is filled with more tubes than you could imagine. Some have small testicles with no extra plumbing at all.

Some guys have balls that drop low in their scrotum. Some guys have balls that are quite close to their body. And depending on our body temperature, our activity and our state of arousal, our bollocks also respond in different ways and at different times to each other.

This is just another idea the media might feed you. That we are all supposed to look the same as some sort of perfect size and shape. It is nonsense. Embrace the difference.

36

The size and shape of her vulva, her nipples, her everything is irrelevant.

Finally, your partner's anatomy is going to be different from every other partner you have had or you will have.

There is more detail about this further in the book, but the labia, the fleshy folds of skin that are the first thing you see on your partner's genital anatomy, come in all shapes and sizes. Some of these folds are quite long, and some are quite short. Everyone is different. There isn't a 'correct' size and shape. There isn't a perfect labia, just as there isn't the perfect sized cock and perfect sized balls. Everyone is different. Everyone has different anatomy.

Your nipples, your partner's nipples, your partner's breasts, other partner's nipples and breasts, they are all going to be different. Some people have large nipples, some are small, some have long nipples, some are tiny, some areolas, the area around the nipple, are wide, some are small. Breasts come in all shapes and sizes. They are all glorious. Embrace the difference in the breasts and nipples that arrive in your life.

Your partner's clitoris shape and size is going to be different to anyone else you might have intimate contact with. Everyone's clitoris is glorious. We're all different.

In general you need to practice embracing your and everyone else's differences rather than thinking there is some sort of perfect that you aren't and that you need to fix, or that your partner isn't and she needs to fix.

We are all different and that is one of the wonders of humanity.

37

This next thing is one of the most important bits of information in this book! What is happening in your brain and in your underwear can be two different things.

There will be many times in your life when you get an erection but there is nothing sexy going on in your head. Sometimes it happens when traveling, a bus or train or car, sometimes spontaneously when you are doing the shopping and many times during the night. This will happen when you aren't thinking about sex. The opposite will also sometimes happen, where you are thinking about sex, in fact you might be in a sexy situation, and you can't get an erection.

What is happening in your underwear is different from your brain.

The term for this is 'arousal non concordance' and is one of the things about sex that very few people understand. *(for more detailed information than I am about to go into, read 'Come as you are' by Emily Nagoski, p 189-217.)*

The most important element of this is understanding that this also happens to women. In fact, the non concordance element of what is happening in the brain and what is happening in their underwear is even more extreme in women.

In men, what is happening in the brain and in the genitals is the same 50% of the time. In women, this number is 10%. That's right. 10%. So 10% of the time for women what is happening in the brain and in the genitals is the same thing.

One of the very important consequences of this for you to understand relates to consent. It might be you are having a fumble with someone and their vagina is wet, but they say they don't want to have sex with you. Before you knew this information, you might have been in the position where you would think, 'They're saying no but they are wet, so they must be enjoying it.'

What is happening is that their body is aware that something sex focused is happening, so is turning on their sex mechanisms, getting them wet. But the more important element here is that their brain and their conscious decision is saying they don't want to. So what do you do? You stop.

This lack of understanding of non concordance has often been the defense of blokes who have been accused of sexual assault. The woman they assaulted says they were saying no, but the guy says that they were wet so clearly they wanted it or they wouldn't be wet. This is fundamentally incorrect.

You must listen to the brain and therefore the voice of your partner and what is being said, not what you are feeling in terms of the state of their vaginal moisture.

The opposite may also happen, where your partner is absolutely into whatever you are doing and completely wants to have amazing sex with you but they have little to no vaginal moisture. This is where lubricant is your best friend.

Listen to what is being said, not what you are feeling. Talk about this with as many of your friends as possible. It is extremely important.

38

Using toys as alternatives

Sometimes you might be in a position where you just can't get a rod on, maybe you want to get it on but for some reason you need some help. Or maybe you have finished, and as we discuss elsewhere the sex isn't over and your partner is still flying and wants to go further.

Most of the ideas about toys and sex toys are that dildos and vibrators are for women and owned by women, and those artificial vaginas are for men. Another idea about toys is that they make blokes feel inferior or emasculated. You don't need to feel this way.

What if you had a vibrator or dildo yourself and you bring these out to play when your own cock is having a rest? She is already flying, wants to go further and then you produce more stimulation, more exquisite possibilities for her to just blow her mind.

This could be quite a challenging idea for some of you, that as a bloke you own a vibrator or dildo. But the reality here is, if you brought a partner home, got down to it and then produced one of these and knew how to use it, you would have a very happy partner. Either a dildo or vibrator is fine. There are lots of different materials, like glass and silicone dildos, alongside differently made vibrators. Options are always good.

Obviously, make sure it is clean and sterilized and if you are having an encounter with multiple partners at the same time, make sure every time you change the partner you are pleasuring it with, you stick a condom on it as well to keep everyone safe.

39

Safe Sex

40

Safe sex - It is very simple

This is the part of the book you probably all have the most experience receiving information about, whether at school, or from family or whatever. But we have to remember safe sex isn't just about STI's . Safe sex is about a range of things.

First of all, in this context, what does Safe mean? In terms of STI's it means putting yourself in a position where you aren't going to pick something up or spread something you have. Wear a condom. Simple. Cover your cock so intimate skin contact doesn't happen and therefore sharing of dodgy viruses, bugs, infections etc….. doesn't happen. Also means you won't run the risk of unwanted pregnancy.

If you do have one, then get it sorted out. If you are having sex with anyone while you have an STI, tell them about it, or don't have sex until it is sorted. STI's are much more common than you think, there is just a stigma attached to them which means people don't talk about them. Be smart about it. No-one wants the stigma of being the person who infected others. Get it checked and dealt with.

In terms of unwanted pregnancy, also make sure you don't

touch yourself or have pre-cum on your fingers when you put your fingers inside your partner. Pre-cum is also sperm, and even the smallest amount can wriggle in there and impregnate your partner. You might not even have sex with her, you could just be fooling around, and she could get pregnant. It could also happen the other way. She jerks you off, has cum on her hand or fingers, touches herself and the same outcome happens. Also, the 'pull-out' method is not a method of contraception.

How else might we be defining Safe in this conversation? Safe could mean an environment of care and consideration where the focus is on the two of you and you are emotionally available, intimate and focused solely on each other. Safe could mean there isn't any filming going on, there isn't a chance whatever is being shared between the two of you is going to get out into the world.

Safe could mean you both know whatever happens isn't also going to be discussed with best friends, again what happens between the two of you stays between the two of you.

Safe means you both agreed if something is uncomfortable, if something doesn't feel right, the other will stop. Or the other will listen and be attentive to what your or their needs are.

Physically safe. Emotionally safe. Intimately safe.

Remember, being safe is one of the two rules about sex. Your partner has to feel safe in all definitions of the word and you have to feel safe in all definitions of the word. When you are feeling safe and both of you consent, extraordinary intimate times will be yours.

41

Condoms are your responsibility

Having condoms is your responsibility, not the responsibility of your partner. Don't begin an intimate encounter without being prepared. Don't begin an intimate encounter expecting your partner to have condoms with her. Far too many guys think that being prepared and having a condom is not their responsibility. This is not true. It is your responsibility. And you need to make sure you have more than one for if one fails and also, in an intimate encounter you are probably going to use more than one.

You also need to make sure your condom is in use by date and is made of the right materials for whatever lube you are using. If it is out of date, it will be highly likely to fail. If you use the wrong lube with the condom you are using, it might also fail. For example, oil based lubes break condoms. You need to use a water based one to make sure.

Condoms aren't cheap but you are able to buy them in bulk to keep your costs down, or split the costs between you and your mates or partner to buy in bulk. Having condoms is your responsibility, not the responsibility of your partner.

42

Sex after consuming too much alcohol, smoking too much weed or taking other substances.

You are responsible for your actions when you are drunk or high or both.

This needs repeating. You are responsible for your actions when you are drunk or high or both.

Alcohol isn't responsible. Your friends aren't responsible. The weed or class A's or whatever you are consuming aren't responsible.

You are.

Sex when ripped, mostly through too much alcohol, is potentially problematic for three reasons. The first is if you and your partner are thoroughly hammered then getting a very clear understanding of consent from either of you can be challenging.

A lot of the rape cases seen in the news are clear about the impact of alcohol on decision making or on a lack of information on the decisions of the protagonists, mostly with the women saying there was no consent and the blokes saying there was, but with an enormous amount of alcohol having been consumed. The other problem here is jury bias often moves against the female defendant, suggesting she was at fault for drinking too much. This is fundamentally wrong. The male in this situation shouldn't be pursuing sex when consent isn't 100% clear. I'm also not commenting on all rape cases.

It might be a good idea to ask your female friends if they ever felt uncomfortable around you when you are drunk. Are you a liability when you are drunk? Do they all know not to be near you when you have had a few? Listen to the answer and action what they are telling you.

Second, the lowering of inhibitions that occurs when drinking alcohol or consuming whatever you might consume, can lead you into unsafe behaviour. You might not use a condom, leaving yourself open to a range of STDs you otherwise wouldn't get.

The third reality is excessive consumption of alcohol, weed or narcotics can negatively impact your performance. If you drink too much, the reality is your cock just isn't going to be as hard as it might potentially be. Nothing like a limp dick to spoil the potential good fun you are wanting to get into.

So imagine you have spent the evening successfully engaging with someone you fancy and who clearly fancies you, and then you both happily and excitedly head back to yours or theirs, get into some awesome and steamy action and you can't get hard. Or maybe you can get about 60% hard, but certainly not enough to make your cock actionable. Remember, there are many other ways of having sex without using your cock, but you will still want to have the option. Alcohol will likely take that option away.

There is a similar impact with weed, although not as dramatic, and with more consumption comes more limp possibilities.

With class A drugs there are a variety of impacts. There is a great irony with Ecstasy, as the reason people use it is it supposedly makes you feel very good and touch is augmented in many different ways, but the reality is it impedes your ability to get hard and sustain it. Speed does something similar in terms of getting and sustaining an erection, but without the touch brought on by Ecstasy.

Cocaine seems to impact people in different ways, but one of the challenges with Cocaine is it puts you in a state of mind to make completely wrong decisions. It amps arrogance and makes you ignore the reality of your situation, meaning you may well regret choices you make, not just sexually but also taking risks you shouldn't be taking, like also not wearing a condom when you should as you think you are impervious to harm. Heroin and opioids also have a negative effect on your manhood.

The biggest impacts of alcohol, weed, class A drugs? They help us lower our inhibitions. And obviously different substances impact people in different ways. Some people are lovable after a few drinks. Others are angry and others are fighty. And if they take something else, the impact will continue to change. The point is be aware that getting hammered, while lowering your inhibitions, may also lower your potential for a good night in. And considering this book is all about how we can be the best we can be in sexual situations, getting lathered does the opposite to you.

The reality of alcohol in particular on your female partner is also generally the more she consumes the more impact there is on how much moisture she produces when she is aroused. Alcohol has a drying effect on the vagina, and while she may be aroused mentally, she may be challenged to take you if you don't have lubricant. This is not a pleasant sensation and if she is too dry for comfortable sex, it will hurt while in the act and will probably continue to hurt for a day if not two days. Something to keep in mind. But if you are too limp and she is too dry, then maybe you want to sleep it off and explore morning sex when you wake up instead, when you are sober, all is working as it should be and consent won't be caught up in an inebriated state of mind.

You can imagine the scenario, I'm sure most guys have thought this through. When you wake up in the morning, you're feeling a little worse for wear from the previous night. You roll over and see you are sharing a bed with someone. You have vague recollections of the previous night, of the fun you had, bringing this person home and having sex with them. This might be a one night stand, this might be someone you are seeing or have a regular sex buddy relationship with.

So the question here is, what is going to happen when she wakes up, also recollects the night and starts to put some things together. Do you remember whether she was totally up for sex? Was she actually in a state to make a choice about whether you had sex? Maybe she was up for it and in a state to make this decision. What if she can't quite remember, maybe through the fog of a hangover she remembers she wasn't too sure about sex with you, maybe she remembers asking you to stop because she wasn't up for it, was too inebriated and just wanted to go to sleep. Does she remember whether you stopped? Or did you keep going because you were so close to finishing you stupidly just kept on going?

This is the kind of scenario you need to put yourself through before you decide to get lathered and start having sex and then not remembering the reality of the evening events. It is your responsibility to yourself and to your partner to be in a frame of mind to know what is going on and to act if things change. Most of us have been so drunk we don't remember the reality of what happened to us. Indeed some people completely forget hours of their lives. Some of this is a convenience. They pretend to have amnesia but they are actually just embarrassed about what they did. For others though this is real. And if this is truly real for you, and something happened where you forced your partner into sex they didn't want to have and you don't remember what happened, then you are in for some serious problems.

Finally, the reality of limp equipment and not being sober enough to really know what you are doing is going to result in you being pretty poor in bed. In this situation the feeling of suddenly not being able to get it up can be challenging and humiliating. You have other choices obviously, your tongue and fingers can work wonders and you don't need your cock to give your partner a good time. And the reality is you are unlikely to have hand and tongue dexterity when hammered, alongside the feeling of embarrassment of not getting hard.

You have a couple of choices here. First of all, don't get so hammered you can't get hard, don't know what you are doing and can't respond to requests from your partner, both to continue what you are doing or to change or to stop. Enjoy yourself, consume whatever you are going to consume, but don't hit your limiter if you are wanting to get it on later.

The other option is if you are too lathered, make a decision not to do the deed that night, while you are still hammered. Make an agreement to sleep instead and then get it on in the morning.

Morning sex is underrated and there is something to be said for waking up sober, still massively fancying the person you are sleeping with, so beer goggles haven't distorted your sense of reality, knowing they are also up for it and then spending several hours in the morning doing what would have finished in 10 minutes the night before.

There is also a reality that in this scenario your potential partner will be super respectful of your decision not to get it on the night before. This kind of restraint is rare, so to demonstrate it, to show restraint the night before, can pay massive dividends the morning after.

Lastly, let's think about the scenario where someone is drunk, you really fancy them, but their drunken state means you turn them down, because having read all the above, you don't want to put yourself in a potentially problematic situation.

How do you do this without shaming her? How can you be careful and kind and gentle with your No, rather than brutal and abrupt and shaming? Remember what it feels like to be rejected? Don't place this feeling on someone else.

Going out and having a good time doesn't mean you can't have amazing intimate sex with someone. You just have to be aware that consumption of alcohol or drugs can make consent unclear and can also inhibit your performance. If you think this might happen, hold the satisfying of your intense desires until the following morning, when you are sober and will find the morning after sex far more satisfying than the potentially drunk fumble of the night before.

43

Anal Sex

Anal sex isn't taboo, and isn't wrong and isn't negative. Anal sex can be extraordinary, feel phenomenal for both partners, be safe, be mind blowing and brilliant. But there are things about it you have to take into consideration.

Directly from the porn industry we have the desire of most guys to have anal sex with their partner. And we have a population of women who are being bombarded by guys wanting to do this, and they don't want to. Some do, some love it and get great pleasure from it, but the majority don't. Ask yourself the question, would you be interested in being the recipient of anal sex? Now have a good think about your answer.

None of what comes up next is meant to scare you away. This is just information you might want to know and will help with having an amazing time.

The first reality you will have to deal with is this. If you are having anal sex, you might get shat on. Most of the porn stars in the films where they have anal sex will have given themselves enemas before filming and they will have eaten very little the night before to limit what they produce the following day. So they essentially flush themselves clean before they start, so they won't shit themselves on screen and their male partner won't get shit on his cock.

This doesn't mean it won't or doesn't happen. And you can be guaranteed if it did happen, it wouldn't make the final edit, unless the film they are making is about a shit fetish. If your partner hasn't given herself an enema or cleaned herself up, be prepared to have shit all over your cock. And if this is the case and you are exploring all of this in bed, you should also put some towels down, just to catch any unexpected spillage.

Secondly, there is no lubrication in the anus. Frankly, the anus is designed to push matter out from the inside, not to be penetrated from the outside in. The constant stretching of the anal sphincters, the muscles supporting the anal opening, can have a permanently disabling impact. There are numerous current and former porn stars who wear sanitary pads on an almost permanent basis as they no longer have physical control of these muscles, meaning they can't close their arsehole when they are busting to go, and instead they permanently leak.

This is basically because they have been hammered in the arse so much, and mostly by abnormally hung blokes, meaning the muscles are permanently damaged.

If you are going to have anal sex with your partner, and obviously they happily consent to it, then make sure you have enough lubricant. You don't want to get yourself in there and for it to be dry. The reality of thrusting and a dry environment is you might split your foreskin or you split the internal skin of their anus, or you split their arsehole itself. The last thing you want to happen is any of this. Having a wound on your cock or in their arse, then being exposed to the bacteria in the arse, is going to have a very unpleasant impact on healing..

Be super aware of how your partner is feeling when you are having sex in this way, as if they are feeling a little under pressure then they might also not tell you they aren't enjoying themselves or even more so, that it hurts and they want you to stop. This is where your super spidey sense for knowing the reality of how your partner is responding comes into play. Yes, you can be enjoying every minute of having your cock in your partner's arse, but if she isn't enjoying it, then you have to stop. Simple.

As I wrote above, there will be women who love anal sex. There are incredibly pleasurable areas in the arse area, and finding and exploring these can be amazing. But also remember just because they enjoy it today doesn't mean they want to do it tomorrow.

Everything changes every time we have an intimate experience with our partners. You are different today from yesterday, they are also different today from yesterday. You must be open to this at all times.

A couple of extras when it comes to anal sex. You obviously know this is where we evacuate our waste. The reality is the bacteria and flora in the rectum is complex, and also not supposed to go anywhere else. So you might have seen porn where the guy pulls his cock out of his partner's arse, and then sticks it in her mouth or her vagina.

This, fellas, is a really bad idea. If you want your partner to have the potential for a whole host of infections in her mouth and vagina, then go right ahead and do this. But really, just don't. You will be transferring serious unpleasantness from where it is supposed to be, to where it absolutely should not be. If you have been exploring anal sex with a condom and want to get back to vaginal sex, take your condom off and put a new condom on.

Finally, there are numerous erogenous zones in the arse, nerve endings that feel good when being nudged by a cock. It also might be that the movement of the cock in the arse is in such a way the nerves of the vagina and wider clitoris are also being rubbed.

There are also options where you can use a vibrator on your partners clitoris and/or vagina while having anal sex with her, to enhance all the sensations she can experience. So anal sex isn't taboo, and isn't wrong and isn't negative. Anal sex can be extraordinary, feel phenomenal for both partners, be safe, be mind blowing and brilliant. But there are things about it you have to take into consideration.

Finally, don't put anything in the ass that doesn't have a wider base than the shaft. The ass will literally suck it up and a trip to A&E will be necessary. So make sure there is a stopper or base to your ass-focused dildo or vibrator.

The point of this little chapter is to be clear that anal sex has been sold to you by porn as a normal part of sex for everyone and all women think it is fine. It isn't. It is a normal part of sex for some women who like it, but a majority of women don't, and you need to respect their wishes.

Finally, I think you should be prepared to experience what you are wanting your partner to experience. Anal sex isn't just for porn or for gay men. Who says you might not love it? Anal play from fingers can be deeply pleasurable, particularly if your partner is able to stroke your prostate gland. With a little more at stake are you prepared to have your partner put on a strap-on and for you to receive? You might find you have never asked yourself this question, as the idea of it is so foreign. You might recoil in horror at the idea. You might try it and you might love it. You won't know unless you try.

If you are shocked by this suggestion, then how do you think your partner will respond to this request? You might be excited by the idea. If so, tell her and have the experience. You might love it, you might hate it, but at least you have been prepared to give it a go. This is a part of intimacy, a part of sharing yourself with someone you really want to be with.

Remember, when it comes to sex there are really only two rules. Is it safe, in all the various ways, and is it consensual? Within these rules, everything is possible.

44

Period sex

There still seems to be a taboo about having sex with your partner if she is on her period. This seems to be a throwback to medieval thinking, some thinking that also still exists in various corners of the world suggesting women are somehow 'dirty' and 'unclean' when they are having their period. This is nonsense. Sex while your partner is having her period can be amazing, and also a little scary when you see your cock covered in blood. But it is worth doing for a couple of reasons.

The first and most important is your actions are clearly saying her menstruating isn't something that is going to stop you doing what you normally do. You are saying it isn't an inhibitor to your normal activities and she isn't 'dirty' or 'unclean' etc.... Nonsense perpetuated by our often small minded world. She knows this already, but sometimes the voices saying this nonsense are loud and get under your skin. Your actions negate them.

Next, blood is a natural lubricant. Her menstruating is giving you a natural lubricant in all the best ways, meaning sex is going to be supported by a seriously helpful slipperiness.

Sometimes blood all over your cock and lower abdomen can look as though you have seriously damaged yourself but can obviously be rectified by a shower. I would also suggest putting towels down if you don't want to sleep in blood. Or have sex in the shower.

There is a heightened sense of touch and response to touch for women during their period, and this extra sensitivity can be something you can enhance. Each person is different, but my suggestion is that at the beginning of any sexual adventure while your partner is on her period, you should be a little softer or lighter with your initial touch, as any heavy touch could be too much and turn her off as it could be uncomfortable. Start lighter, ascertain what is positive and pleasurable for her and go from there. You and she might find her orgasms are heightened and the journey to pleasure will be increased in awe-inspiring ways. The muscular contraction from orgasm can also relieve period pain as it can help relax the muscles causing the pain.

There is also a heightened susceptibility to infection when she is on, so it is also important to be vigilant about being safe in all your actions.

The reality is that if your partner is challenged by her period and doesn't enjoy those days of her life, which can be the case, you can possibly help this situation by making sex during menstruation a regular thing, ensuring you focus on making sure she feels incredible. This focus on creating a positive, exciting and pleasurable experience when she is normally feeling the opposite way could potentially be an extraordinary emotional and physical help to her. Don't underestimate what the impact of this could be. But likewise, this could be the worst suggestion in the world if nothing can change the unpleasantness some menstrual cycles cause. At least trying and being clear about wanting to do something that makes her feel better will be a good start.

45

Lube is your Friend

Following on from Anal Sex and Period sex, one of the best ideas you can work with, across all areas of the sex you have, is that lubricant is your friend, and lubricant will make everything better than you can possibly imagine.

Sometimes the use of lubricant can feel like a negative thing to do. For example, if I use lube that means she isn't wet enough, therefore turned on enough, therefore she isn't really interested, therefore I'm a bit rubbish with this sex thing or she doesn't like me........ you get the idea. We can all go down this rabbit hole very quickly and it isn't helpful.

The best idea you can work with is this. Just use lubricant. Just use it. There are no special reasons. Just use lubricant. She will love what you do even more. You will love what you do even more. Happy days for all involved.

Do warm it up before you apply it, unless you like to put it on cold as it is mostly cold. This can be an interesting temperature change and can feel surprisingly good. But unless you know she likes this, warm it up first.

And while you might think once you have applied lubricant

you probably can't go down on her because you will get lube in your mouth and it won't taste very nice, it is best to get over yourself and leave the option open. It does have an 'interesting' taste, but if you go down on her like an expert and are using lube as well, she will be very happy.

Finally, there are lots of different lubes available, so there might be some ingredients you or your partner might get irritated by, and there are also lubes that aren't compatible with condoms as they cause the condom to disintegrate. Make sure you are using a lube that is right for you both and is also right for your condoms.

46

Casual sex isn't casual sex - the emotional impact of sex is real.

The casualness of sexual encounters in our world has now got to a point where there is a real misunderstanding of the emotional impact having sex with someone can have. When we have dating apps guiding us to hook up with people for 'quick and meaningless sex', it can lead to a feeling of sex being a physical act with no impact other than making us blow our load after being in the intimate company of someone.

Perhaps the idea of a casual sex buddy is one people are interested in? Maybe the idea they can call a friend when feeling a little horny, meet up, sort each other out then continue with their lives with no long term impact on either of them is something that is enticing? This might sound like a perfect situation, but the reality is there is always an impact on people when having casual sex.

You might have hooked up with someone half a dozen times, had a drink, maybe a dinner date, great sex etc...... but you think this is just the two of you enjoying each other's company and not getting emotionally involved. This most likely won't be true. Sometimes it will, but it is better you understand it is more than likely if you are having casual sex with someone, emotionally one of you or both of you are going to be impacted.

I know several guys who have had casual partners, got a bit bored with them and decided they liked their casual partner's friend. Thinking there wasn't anything emotional or committed with their current casual sex partner, without thinking about it they pursued the friend. An extraordinary cluster of problems ensued, with the guys realising, mostly because they were being shouted at by their previous partner, that this new situation wasn't okay. They thoroughly screwed someone's friendship, often with a best friend, alongside leaving their previous partner miserable and broken hearted.

They thought it was casual. It was to begin with, but it became something more for the partner involved. I have also known this situation in reverse. The girl in the partnership has fancied a friend of the casual partner and gone for him. All hell breaks loose as the guy makes it very clear to the girl that through their casual sexual encounters he has actually fallen in love with her and she has just broken his heart.

We are often still so reserved about sharing our feelings with others, mostly for self preservation and because we hold our most treasured and vulnerable secrets close to ourselves. And when we are falling in love with someone, there is always the fear they won't be feeling the same way toward us. Or maybe there is the fear for ourselves of falling in love, particularly if we have been in love previously and had our hearts broken.

So be careful with casual. Talk through what is going on and be clear about intentions and also if those intentions for casual begin to turn into feelings for more, talk about it with your partner. In case you haven't realised, you can't read minds and no-one can read yours. There are always consequences from intimacy. Always.

Finally, don't Ghost someone. Be big enough to talk to them if you don't want to see them again. Ghosting someone is just being an asshole. Don't be an asshole. Treat people with respect, even if you don't like them anymore.

47

Premature Ejaculation

There is a misconception among a significant proportion of the population that as a male in a sexual encounter you should be able to 'last' for a long time, and if you don't you have a problem and suffer from Premature Ejaculation. I have read on forums guys talking about suffering from premature ejaculation, then going on to say they lasted 20 minutes.

Let's get a grip on reality here. The average amount of time a guy lasts while having penetrative sex is about 2 ½ minutes. Not 20 minutes, not 2 hours. It is a natural response to stimulation, intimacy and all the elements of a sexual encounter you are going to bubble up and blow quite quickly.

Allied to this is you will have probably conditioned yourself, because of your masturbatory tactics of knocking one out as quickly as possible, to ejaculate as fast as possible, as we discussed in chapter 18

There are a range of things you can do here, and everything in this book is here to help you. And before we begin, this entirely normal quickness of shooting your load can be very frustrating for your partner if you have spent no time in foreplay, in exploring her and in focusing on her pleasure.

Firstly, take your time when masturbating. Train yourself to last longer. Most importantly, take your time in your foreplay. Take your time in focusing on her pleasure and exploring what helps her feel incredible. Ensure she is having a wonderful time with you.

Then, if and when you are having penetrative sex, take your time. If you feel like you are heading toward an end point, but don't want to, then slow down or stop. You want to minimise the stimulation of both your cock and your skin, because this is going to be sending messages to your brain as much as your bell end. Then start again. And stop again. And repeat.

Every time will be different. Sometimes you won't be able to help yourself but ejaculate quickly. Remember, sex isn't finished when you are. So if you have finished quickly, keep exploring her, keep supporting her pleasure. Sometimes you might last for half an hour. Sometimes you might not even ejaculate. This is also fine. Every time is different.

Don't place ludicrous boundaries and rules on what should or shouldn't happen. Be in the moment. Focus on your partner and her pleasure.

48

Slapping and Rough sex

49

Slapping and strangling your partner is not what happens in 'normal' sex

There is a growing trend of guys slapping and strangling their partners while engaging in sex. In reading extensively of this in online forums where women are discussing this, the conclusion is that it is an outcome of watching porn.

Slapping and strangling your partner while engaging in sex is not a part of a 'normal sexual experience'. The use of the word 'normal' here is challenging, as there is no normal, but slapping and strangling is a very particular 'kink' or 'action' enjoyed by a very small percentage of the population. (If you are into kink or different sexual adventures, there are numerous communities online you can join and be a part of and will guide you through the ways and means of what you want to explore. Remember, the only rules are consent and being safe.)

The slapping doesn't just mean slapping the face, it also means slapping the butt, the legs, the breasts: essentially any part of the body of the woman you are having sex with.

Strangling your partner is enjoyed by an even smaller percentage of the population. It is unclear in the use of this in porn whether this is being done as a power position for the male involved, or if it is in some way trying to give the female partner an experience of sexual asphyxiation, where breathing is restricted to heighten orgasm.

If your partner is interested in being slapped, then talk to her about where on her body she would like it to happen and in what part of your intimate session she thinks it will support her sensation.

If she is interested in asphyxiation then do your research online to ensure you are safe and you don't cause her injury. There are plenty of people who have died as a result of trying sexual asphyxiation and getting it wrong, both masturbating and also with partners. Remember, nothing is out of bounds within intimate sessions, as long as you have consent and you are being safe.

Finally, beginning to slap your partner and/or strangle your partner while in the middle of a session and without having discussed it beforehand is seriously not OK. You haven't gained consent for this particular activity, nor have you discussed safety if you are playing with strangling. So the reality here is that you are actually assaulting your partner.

Finally, as with all kinks involving pain, domination and submission or even just something different, you must have a safe word you both know and both agree to use to indicate you have had enough and want to stop with whatever it is you are doing. Again, this is another part of consent and through agreement you need to ensure both parties involved feel confident they can stop any action at any time.

50

Rough Sex

Rough sex is another one of these sexual 'activities' influencing the way men engage in sex and something you must be very aware of and careful with. This is another result of the influence of porn and another demonstration of how what used to be considered more 'hard core' porn has become normalised.

Sometimes in a sexual encounter your activity levels get massively heightened, you are both being very physical and are both getting potentially a little bit 'rougher' with your movements, both individually and together. The rough sex in this chapter isn't this. When this happens it is usually because you have both arrived at the same place together and the extra physical pressure together is very exciting and stimulating.

The rough sex I am talking about is where you start to get very physical with your partner, throwing her up and down on the bed, slamming her pelvis as hard as possible every time you thrust and generally causing what is easily described as bodily harm. There are numerous postings on forums of women not being able to sit down after this kind of sex as they are too bruised and battered from being smashed in the pelvis, had a bruised cervix, some were bleeding for a couple of days. These women described their experiences as deeply unpleasant, painful and scary. They are also clear they found the experience frightening, and they were too frightened to ask for it to stop.

Rough sex has become the defense of choice for guys who have been charged with murder or manslaughter of their partners. They suggest in their defence that they were having rough sex and it went wrong. This is a very challenging topic, and this book doesn't have the scope to go into it, but needless to say it is clear these have been violent, vicious men who are hiding behind this defence.

There may be some women who enjoy rough sex, and enjoy being thrown around and the violence of it. This is something that must be discussed before you have sex. Suddenly going from vigorous and fantastic sex you are both enjoying to throwing her around and causing potential serious bodily harm is not OK. It is assault.

However, as with everything else in this book, if your partner is into being thrown around and having intensely rough sex, and you have a safe word you both know and respect and will stop you in the middle of all your action if needed, then go ahead and explore.

Remember, there are two rules. Consent and safety. Everything else is up to you and your partner.

51

Revenge Porn - Sharing your sexual life with mates….. Please don't……

Revenge porn is a truly horrible part of our world. Filming your sex life to ensure you can totally mess your partner's life up if they leave you or it all goes horribly wrong. This is awful and wrong. Sometimes revenge porn is filmed with the intention of using it in this way. But sometimes it isn't.

Perhaps the initial intent will be to film yourselves so you can look back at it and enjoy the memory of an epic session of awesome sex. It might be this is a one off film, or maybe either you or both of you enjoy the experience and the view later and you film yourself again, and again. (By the way, filming someone in a private situation without their consent is illegal and the consequences are significant. There we have Consent again).

And then the relationship turns sour. Things start to go wrong, you stop liking each other and you go your separate ways. Bad things are said. Both of you are hurt emotionally and both of you want to get the other back for what they said or did. So then you decide to publicly humiliate your former girlfriend by sharing the film of your sexual adventures either with mates or with the world online. Pretty guaranteed if you share it with your mates. If you don't put it online, then one of them will.

So now the world can see one of your most intimate moments, and because you posted it against her will and without her consent, she is humiliated. The world sees her, and you, at your most vulnerable. And the internet being what it is, this is never taken down. It is not removable, because there are people and organizations who search for, find and save this stuff.

Don't do it guys. If you are tempted, delete the footage. Delete all evidence and history of anything that happened so you can't fall into the trap of posting it when you might have had a couple of drinks too many or are feeling particularly angry and unable to make clear decisions. You might also leave your phone around and your mates could search, find something and post it to themselves.

Finally, the conversations with your mates about your sex life. This is a personal choice, but what you get up to when you are having an intimate moment isn't anyone else's business. . Privacy is important and we have less and less of it than we used to. Shield your privacy for yourself and your partner.

Others disagree and think sharing this stuff with friends is a definition of a solid friendship. Just be aware that your intimate moments shared with a few select friends, particularly if the action you are talking about was super hot, may not stay with those select friends for very long. And having all this as public knowledge can be tough to take and if it ends up online, it will never go away.

52

Dick pics…… really….?

You have the opportunity for a relationship with someone, they like you, you like them, it is getting interesting, sharing messages, some photos of yourself etc. So why does everyone think it is OK to send dick pics? Really? It doesn't 'show her what she's missing'. It doesn't 'Get her horny to want it'. She doesn't 'imagine it inside her'. The reality here guys is when she has received a dick pic, she will eye roll, sigh, shout loudly and then stop speaking to you or know you're 'that kinda guy' and will probably make sure everyone of her friends avoid you.

If she says, send me a photo of your cock, then maybe, but maybe the response could be she can see it live if she is interested?

If you think you want her to get a good look at your cock, show her in person, when it's appropriate of course. If it doesn't happen, then be thankful she never got a look in the first place. I have had plenty of conversations with women who said they were clearly interested in the bloke they were communicating with until he sent a dick pic. If these guys had kept it in their trousers, they were much more likely to end up having a very hot time.

I think blokes think the women they are communicating with want to see a photo of their dick. Most don't. Some might, but the majority really don't. They don't want to see your knob unless they are super interested in getting intimate and really only ever in person when action is about to happen. Then they get to see it live and this is where the reveal should happen.

53

Control, Power and Unrealistic Expectations

54

Just because you compliment a woman, doesn't mean she is therefore indebted to you.

An odd attitude of a range of men is if they compliment a woman, on her dress, how she looks, something she does, she is somehow indebted to them and therefore owes them something.

The sense of this is if I say you look amazing, you will come and have a drink with me. If I say you look nice, you have to automatically accept the compliment. If I say something nice and if you don't react positively towards me for noticing you then you're a bitch and deserve to be sworn at.

And this happens a lot. A bloke makes an unwanted comment to a woman, the woman ignores him and continues on her way and the guy gets aggressive, calling her a bitch and a slut and threatening all sorts of violence.

This is more normal than you might think. This also happens a lot when there are a group of men around, often the friends of the guy making the comment. So not only is it threatening just having one guy in their face, but suddenly having 2,3 or 4 being aggressive is very frightening.

This isn't OK.

You don't have some 'right' to a response, just because you have complimented someone on their outfit, their hair, or whatever you think you might compliment her on.

You need to also be aware of your mates who might do this. Call them on their behaviour. The more of you there are out there not tolerating this behaviour, and being vocal about it, the less likely it will happen.

55

Telling her how she should manage her lady garden is not on.

How your partner chooses to present her intimacy to you is none of your business. If she wants to shave herself, her choice. If she wishes to grow her pubic hair so she could plait 3-foot ponytails , this is her choice. If she wants to shave the image of her favourite musician into her pubic hair, again her choice.

The idea that female intimate areas should be shaved is another impact of porn where the vast majority of women are shaved bare. What your partner does with it is none of your business. Unless she asks for your opinion and your design input. Then tell her, you have permission. But not before.

There are countless tales I have read of girls having an early sexual encounter only for the guy to point at her crotch, which might have some hair on it, cry EUWWWW! What the hell is that!!!

This is due to the fact there is hair there, and this action makes the girl feel like absolute shit. The consequence of this kind of action on the girl is unfathomable. Imagine you pull your cock out and your girlfriend squeals and points at it and shouts 'what is that thing??? Get it away from me it's awful' Won't make you feel particularly attractive now will it?

So again, your opinion on how she presents herself to you is not required. The fact you are with her and about to get intimate, and you have an opportunity to have amazing sex with her ? This is all you should be focusing on.

And if because of your porn habits you think all women should be shaved bare, maybe something for you to try is to shave your own pubic hair then experience the discomfort of it growing back. Itchy, uncomfortable and just not very nice. And similarly to her choices, what you also do to your pubic hair is your business and no-one else's.

What she does with her pubic hair is none of your business.

56

Don't ask her if she orgasmed. Just don't.

Guys, don't ask her if she orgasmed. If she has you will know. If she hasn't, you will also know. If you ask and she says no, what are you going to do? Are you prepared for this? Guys ask this because they want their partner to tell them what a thumping stud he is and how good he is in bed.

If she wants to tell you she came 10 times, this is her choice. If she wants to tell you she lost count of her orgasms, then this is her choice. She might also tell you she didn't and you need to think about what you are doing. Keep reading.

Don't ask.

57

Incels and the assumption sex is your right.

The incel 'movement' has gathered pace over the past couple of years and has produced some frightening young men who have clearly been willing to kill others in the name of their movement and to back their political stance.

As can be read across almost everything else in this book, sex with women is not your right, just because you are a male. Sex with a woman is an extraordinary joy and privilege when shared as intimate experience, and is something to be nurtured.

The reasons guys self-select themselves into this group is they aren't successful with having sex with women. And the questions guys who regard themselves as incels are asking as to why this is happening, and the answers they are getting back, are fundamentally wrong.

The incel community squarely blame this whole situation on women. It is women's fault, and in particular feminism, they aren't having sex.

The reason incels aren't having sex isn't down to women. It is because those self-selecting as part of this group are not desirable for a woman to have sex with and probably aren't desirable for a woman to have even a non sexual relationship either. I am in no way trying to shame anyone here. If you have tried a range of times to engage in a relationship with different women and nothing has come of it, you need to ask yourself some questions.

So the questions needing to be asked revolve around 'How do I become desirable to women?' alongside the basic question of 'What do I need to change to become desirable to women?' There are a few areas.

Conversational ability / personality - When you talk to someone how do you represent yourself? Are you intensely shy? Do you come across as angry or potentially aggressive? Do you muddle your words, get tongue tied and generally say the wrong thing? This is where you need friends who are prepared to be honest with you. If you come across as aggressive but don't realise it, then no wonder women don't want to spend time with you. But if you don't realise it, then you won't be able to do something about it. Find a friend who is prepared to be honest with you. If possible a female friend or acquaintance. Listen to their response and act on it.

Looks: This isn't some sort of handsomeness measurement but more basic things. Are your clothes clean? Is your hair clean? Do you clean your teeth? Do you look like you take care of yourself? In the world of sitting in front of your games console for hours on end, you might think the jeans you have been in for 4 weeks and the shirt you haven't changed for 4 days is fine, but this is not going to interest someone of the opposite sex. Be clean. Eat well. If you look like you can't take care of yourself properly then you certainly won't look like you can take care of someone else.

Interests: Do you sit in front of your computer for hours on end? Do you have no other hobbies or interests apart from games online? Unless she is similarly minded, you aren't going to be interesting to spend much time with. Variety in experience creates variety in conversation, different viewpoints of the world and an interest in things outside yourself.

Attention: Are you actually interested in people you are talking to? Or do you just sit waiting for a gap to jump into with your own opinions? People who don't actually listen to what others say rarely get to round 2 of dating or of conversation. When was the last time you shut up and properly listened to what someone was telling you? And then spent the whole conversation asking them about them? Try this and see what happens.

Positivity vs Negativity: are you feeling beaten up by the world and do you wear this on your sleeve with every encounter you have? Negativity, pessimism and a worldview full of doom and gloom are not sexy traits in anyone. This doesn't mean don't have these feelings, but be aware if this is what you are constantly presenting, then it is going to be a very large barrier for people to get over to wanting to be with you.

For women to want to have sex with you you need to pass several tests. They are a mix of conscious and unconscious and they are tests asking a range of things. These tests will come in questions they will ask themselves, consciously and unconsciously. Some of these might be: When I am with him do I feel safe? Physically and emotionally? Is he clean and does he look after himself? Is he interesting to be with? Am I interested in spending more time with him? Is he the kind of guy I am prepared to get intimate with? Does he make me laugh? Is he genuinely interested in me?

Everything described above can be worked on and developed. Eat well and do some exercise, clean your clothes, your home and yourself on regular occasions, do more interesting things with your life and your interests and above all, listen to what people are saying and respond to them with interest.

If you are in this position where you are struggling with relationships with women, sexual or not, then maybe your environment needs changing. Are you in a group of friends where your culture excludes women and where you have habits described above? Change your friends and make decisions to move in a different direction. This won't be easy, but if you truly want to explore intimacy with women, you might have to make some tough decisions. It is truly worth it.

Finally, personality is more important than looks. You could be the most extraordinary looking guy on the planet, but if you are a total tool, an aggressive wanker with an ego the size of a planet, no one will be interested. But you can be an 'average' looking guy, who is funny, interested, intellectually curious and fun to be around, and you are going to be more successful with women than most men.

We all know guys out there who are incredibly successful with women, guys who are not handsome, are not built like athletes, are not chiseled and 'alpha male' looking but nonetheless seem to have some magnetic quality that attracts women. This magnetic quality is the way they hold themselves, their confidence, their ability to not be phased by rejection, but also an ability not to keep pursuing someone who isn't interested. They are also positive people. These qualities don't appear overnight. They take time and focus.

You too can do this. You have to focus and commit to it and your life will change for the positive.

58

Finally

Ultimately, sex is awesome. Sex is amazing and mind-blowing and transcendent, but sex can also be exposing, humiliating and destructive.

Intimacy and a desire to share yourself in a range of ways, to focus on your partner's needs and to commit to giving her an incredible time, all the time, will lead to profound sexual experiences.

59

Part 2

60

Introduction to Part 2

The next part of this book is about what you should think about in preparation for intimacy, what to do to be brilliant in bed and a range of exercises to help you be more articulate with your hands and touch.

There is a LOT of information here, and the most important thing about this LOT of information is you mustn't become overwhelmed by it.

You might read through it and think there is too much to think about, to consider, to be aware of to be successful. Keep breathing, keep reading, and take your time.

Everything in this chapter will take a little bit of time to understand and practice to get better at. Some of the other elements, like what you can do before anything intimate happens, will be aha moments that will become part of your normal daily routine.

Don't be overwhelmed. There is lots of information. Step by step.

And finally, before we get started, there are elements of this section that might read as a bit 'serious', and not 'fun'. It is serious. It is important you get the information you need without putting it in 'fun' or 'jokey' ways. This isn't a chat with your favourite uncle down the pub. This isn't a chat with your school biology teacher. We're blokes, and sometimes when we need important information about an important matter, we don't want anything extra apart from this information. Sometimes this information can come across as serious.

Remember, everything that follows will make your sex life an incredible adventure.

61

Techniques and Exercises to be amazing in the Bedroom

Remember, no-one tells you how to be amazing in bed. There are no lessons, no proper guides apart from this one. Yet you are expected to know what to do, how to do it and how to be a bedroom master without any information. This is ridiculous. Below is the guide to helping you to achieve master status.

Let's start with some simple rules taking us back to the beginning of the book and the reality that awesome sex with a partner goes hand in hand with respect for that partner and for women in general.

If you start your sexual adventures with trying to emulate porn, you pull your cock out of your trousers and just expect to be sorted out, you aren't going to create a long-lasting sexual partnership, nor is it going to be a demonstration of respect. If your partner likes to start your liaisons like this, and you have had the conversations about consent, it is a different thing. I'm talking about the expectation you will be 'serviced' and you don't care about her.

The focus of these exercises and techniques is purely on

how you engage with, touch, stroke, etc…, and do everything you possibly can with your partner to augment her pleasure in your sexual adventures. If you are sitting reading this and thinking, but what about me? Then you have to trust me. If you practice and are successful in even 30% of the techniques and exercises written below, you will have a mind-blowing time, as your partner is going to be flying with pleasure and will be wanting to give back as much as she is getting.

Anatomy lesson

The anatomy of your partner's Genitals. Where is everything?

One of the trickiest elements of exploring intimacy is knowing where everything is that you are going to be touching, and not fumbling about trying to 'find' anything.

Below is a diagram of the female genital anatomy. Have a look and learn what you need to learn. The most important element here is that you know where the head of the clitoris is. It is quite small, even when aroused, so you need to know where it is in order to find it easily and without fumbling. If you haven't had the experience of being in contact with this part of the clitoris yet, then knowing about where it is before you try to find it will massively enhance your first experiences.

AROUSED

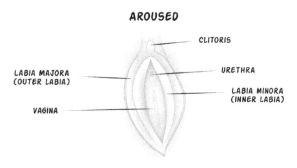

Female Vulva

Despite what you might hear or read, the picture above is not of the vagina, but of the Vulva. The entrance of the vagina is part of the vulva. When your partner is aroused, the different elements of the vulva get engorged with blood, similar to you and your cock. In particular, the head of the clitoris, or glans clitoris, gets bigger and more accessible. The point on the picture above of the Clitoris is the same as the Glans Clitoris below.

THE STRUCTURE OF THE CLITORIS

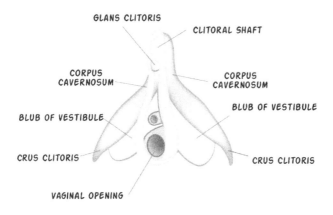

Structure of the Clitoris

In 2009 the first 3D sonograph of the clitoris was made and what it revealed is the clitoris is not the little fleshy button at the top of the vagina everyone used to think it was, but it is a large (10cm long) bulbous organ of beauty that sits deep into the female body as well as wraps around and under the vagina. Considering the number of nerve endings in the Glans, the name of the button-like fleshy wonder at the top of the vagina, sits at around 8000, then we have to wonder what the numbers are across the whole of the organ.

62

Ways to support her pleasure

63

Introduction to orgasm / Introduction to pleasure

Despite the focus of this introduction, of orgasm, I need to remind you that orgasm isn't what you are focusing on as the outcome of your attention when you are being intimate with someone. Your focus is your partner's pleasure. Not their orgasm.

Your partner might be in an incredible state of pleasure, but not have an orgasm. They might be kind of into what you are doing and perhaps not be feeling much pleasure at all, but then orgasm.

Your focus is not on 'getting your partner to orgasm', your focus is on how your attention, in all the different ways you can attend to her, can support her pleasure.

That said, below is an outline of what happens with orgasm, and the very different ways orgasm can occur. It is important to know this, and the process of touch and attention that is described and that may lead to orgasm will form the basis of your focus on her pleasure.

What are the mechanisms happening that lead to orgasm?

First, let's read a quote describing the physiological steps involved in orgasm. This is from an amazing book called 'Come as you are' by Emily Nagoski. I highly recommend you get it and read it cover to cover multiple times.

'Excitement. As stimulation begins, her heart rate, blood pressure, and respiration rate increase, and her labia minora and the clitoris darken and swell, separating the outer labia.

The walls of the vagina begin to lubricate and then lengthen. Her breasts swell and the nipples become erect. Late in excitement, she may begin to sweat.

Plateau. Lubrication begins at the mouth of the vagina, from the Bartholin's glands. Her breasts continue to swell, so much that the nipples seem to retract into the breasts. She may experience "sex flush," a concentration of color over the chest.

By now her inner labia have doubled in size from their resting state. The internal structures of the clitoris lift, drawing the external portion up and inward, so that it retracts from the surface of the body. The vagina itself "tents" around the cervix, open and wide deep inside the body.

She experiences the involuntary muscle contraction known as myotonia, including carpopedal spasms (contraction of muscles in the hands and feet). She may begin to pant or hold her breath, as the thoracic and pelvic diaphragms contract in unison.

Orgasm. All the sphincters of her pelvic diaphragm (the "Kegel" muscle) contract in unison—urethra, vagina, and anus. She experiences rapid breathing, rapid heartbeat, and increased blood pressure. Her pelvis may rock, various muscle groups may tighten involuntarily. She experiences the sudden release of the tension that has accumulated in the muscles throughout her body.

Resolution. Breasts return to baseline, clitoris and labia return to baseline, heart rate, respiration rate, blood pressure all return to baseline."

Understanding the processes leading to her orgasm, the range of factors, all the different ways it can happen, what you do to help this happen, what to do if you are a little uncertain…… will bring you to a whole new dimension. This knowledge, and then the successful practice of this knowledge, will fundamentally change your life. Again, this isn't for you to focus on getting her to orgasm, but your actions to get her there will give her pleasure in a range of ways,

There are a range of different ways you can support your partner to orgasm, and the very interesting thing about this range of ways is that the different areas of stimulation often have different neural pathways to essentially the same place in the brain, where it all kicks off. So if you are kissing your partner passionately, while stroking her skin with one hand and stimulating her clitoris with the other, there are 3 different sensations kicking off in her brain, all bringing those separate sensations into the same area and multiplying the effect.

But very simply neurologically what makes her orgasm is - Clitoral stimulation, sometimes vaginal stimulation, sometimes cervical stimulation, brain stimulation: happy days if you are able to make two or three of these things happen at the same time.

If you spend a significant amount of time reading online

forums about orgasms and the main actions that will get women to experience them you will generally come up with a list that is headlined by:

1. Oral Sex.
2. Clitoral stimulation.

Notice the absence of Penetration from this list? This is important to repeat. Penetration sometimes produces orgasms, but it is not the main way. So get rid of the porn idea of hammering away at your partner to make her orgasm. It might, but really only after you have explored a multitude of other ways.

The primary focus you really need to be working with is clitoral stimulation, both with your fingers and also with oral sex. In particular you need to be working with the knowledge that although the head of the clitoris is potentially small, the whole organ is 'wishbone' shaped as you can see in the previous diagramme and it wraps around the vagina. It is an amazing organ and is still revealing mysteries. Like the arguments over whether there is actually a G-spot may be redundant as the stimulation of the area where the g-spot is said to be could simply be stimulation of a different part of the clitoris from a different angle. So much to experiment with.

There are many different ways you can create the conditions within which she orgasms. And the more you understand what she likes and responds to, the better your ability to ensure she experiences incredible pleasure every time you are together.

It is super important to remind you there is no one 'fix' or 'trick' to getting your partner to orgasm. There are a range of different actions you can explore with her, resulting in a range of different physiological effects. It is also important to remember that the same moves every time you have sex won't get the same results every time.

Your partner is not and you are not the same person today you were yesterday. And they won't be and you won't be tomorrow. So there is no one-move-sorts-her-all-the-time approach. And even if there was, it would be quite boring after a while. Just going through the motions and hitting the same buttons to get the same effect time after time? No thanks.

A bit of technical detail that will rock your world.

In women, the nervous system linking the clitoris, the vagina and the cervix to the brain are all different. So the clitoris is linked through the pudendal nerve, the vagina is linked through the pelvic nerve and the cervix is linked through three different nerves, the pelvic, the hypogastric and the vagus. This could potentially account for the different sensory experiences people have from stimulation of these different areas, and also the different orgasmic qualities stimulation of each area brings.

Because there are these different nervous systems innervating different parts of your partner's sexual zones, all of these systems could be firing at once. Having all these systems firing at the same time could be the reason why some orgasms can be so momentous and epic.

If you then add how the skin is becomes so sensitive when you touch it, you get this multiplying effect of stimulation that can build and build and build from different areas at different times.

So what this means is when you are having sex with your partner, the more areas you can stimulate in a significant and satisfactory way the greater the range of sensation and the greater the impact this will have and the greater the experience of pleasure.

Do be aware of piling in on your first date with trying to stimulate everything all at once. Doing this is possibly going to overload her. If you are having sex with someone who hasn't really experienced pleasure during sex, then going at it all guns blazing may well be too much to deal with as all of these sensations all at once will be too intense.

The best way of engaging all these areas is with a layered approach. This way you stimulate the nerves by very gently stimulating her clitoris, get her feeling incredible and be consistent with what you are doing so there are no peaks and troughs of the experience, then, while keeping this action going, you bring another action in, so maybe while continuing the clitoral stimulus you start getting your fingers involved, gently find her g-spot and start artfully stimulating her there. You keep going with this until she has maybe her third or fourth orgasm (depending on the impact of your clitoral stimulation) then there are other steps to take. You get what I mean.

What really makes her orgasm

So above you will have read the three particular pleasure areas triggering orgasm, but this isn't what truly makes her orgasm.

Orgasm is a result of a wide range of actions, nerve impulses, feelings and stimulation all adding up over time, sometimes a short time, sometimes a long time, to eventually create the mind-blowing results we want.

Orgasm is a result of a layering of stimulation, experience, the right state of mind for the moment of the experience and pleasure. The right environment: is it safe or maybe it is a risky quicky and the risk enhances the buzz. Are you comfortable? Are you trying to have sex on a cold carpeted floor that is really uncomfortable? Are the lights on and/or bright? Does your touch have the right amount of pressure and control? Not too light, and annoying like a mosquito, not too heavy, like you are giving a brutal sports massage.

Are you getting so horny you are trying to eat her face when you kiss her? Not sexy. Are you kissing her how she likes to be kissed? Much sexier. Don't eat her face..

The layering of environment, feelings of safety and feelings of comfort alongside all the physical aspects of building sexual tension and stimulation all contribute to a sense of relaxation and, ultimately, is what really brings her into that state of pleasure and may create the conditions within which she experiences her orgasm.

If she isn't relaxed, feeling safe and into it and you, pleasure and then orgasm isn't going to happen. Or, if the context is different, maybe she is feeling tense because you are going to get caught, but tense in an exciting and thrilling way, not tense in a turn off way.

The answer is that Orgasm starts and finishes in the brain, and you need to feed the brain with all the different layers supporting this.

64

Before you begin

Environment and comfort

Where is this sexual adventure going to happen? Is it in your bedroom? Her bedroom? Is this her family home and are her parents happy for you to be nailing each other while they are in the house? Or are you trying to be quiet? Is this your house and are your parents happy with the antics happening in your bedroom? Or maybe this is your place and your room. Or her place and her room.

All these things underlie comfort and feelings of safety. In her place, her room, she will probably feel safest. Think about these things as they will inform decisions you make. Are you potentially pressuring her into having sex with you while in her house with her parents there as a bit of a dare to yourself to see if you can? Not good. Not good at all.

Is this in your room? You can manipulate the environment, get lighting going, music on, set up an atmosphere you want. How cold is it in your room? How hot? You want to be able to control all the variables that are going to be distracting to her when you start to get into the intensity of pleasure you are working toward, so being relaxed and up for an incredible and intimate session is the simplest and easiest state for her and you to be in.

Cleanliness

Something often forgotten by heterosexual blokes is cleanliness. Apologies to those of you for whom this doesn't apply.

If you are bringing someone back to yours for sexual adventures does your place, your bedroom, your bed, your cock, your skin, your hair, look clean? Feel clean? Smell clean?

Believe me when I say a massive turn off is for someone to come back to yours and walk into a flat or house that is a tip, into a bedroom where you can't see the floor and to then lie and get intimate on sheets that haven't been changed in a month, let alone a room probably smelling of dirty linen, sweat and shoes. All this does is tell someone that the person they are about to have sex with and get super intimate with doesn't care about being clean, and therefore might be passing something on to them they won't want.

So get yourself in the habit of cleaning and sorting your room and your living arrangements, and get yourself into the habit of changing your sheets regularly, so you know if something happened and out of the blue you unexpectedly bring someone home, you won't be embarrassed by what you are bringing someone to.

Another weird one is people who don't shower every day. Some people just don't, which I think is a bit weird. If you want to be naked rolling around with someone, wouldn't you want to be clean when you did so? And then you can get sweaty and dirty together, but this is something completely different.

This is a habit and is easy to get into. Wash your sheets. Wash your clothes. Wash yourself. Wash your cock. Leave your room every day expecting to bring someone home to have sex that evening. You never know. It may happen.

A serious embarrassment is when you bring someone back to yours and before they walk through your bedroom door they are just about ripping your clothes and their clothes off, then through they walk into your bedroom, take one deep breath and inhale a stench of sweat and feet, look at the stained sheet they are going to be having sex on, and all the hot, hot, sexy feeling they had been building to for a couple of hours is literally turned off like a switch. Like it never actually existed in the first place. She says 'Actually, I have to head back to mine, I've got an early start. See you later...' and then is gone, glad to have avoided having sex in a pigsty, and eager to tell her friends of the close escape she just had.

So if you want to avoid this situation, tidy, clean, prepare. Then when she walks through your door she looks at the state of the place, her brain says, right, this looks good, he is clean and tidy; this means I'm not going to be lying on month old sweat and it is highly likely he is clean as well..... Then she proceeds to tear hers and your clothes off..... Sound like a more fun night? I thought so.

Atmosphere.

The Atmosphere of the environment within which you are going to get it on is massively influential. Maybe you don't care where you have sex as long as you are actually having sex.

This is short-sighted and a small-minded attitude. You don't go to clubs or bars that have bright mall-like strip lighting do you? They are dark and moody or dark and cool. They are dark. The lack of bright light in these places elicits a feeling of mystery, a feeling of potential, a feeling of possibility. This, allied to the music in the place gives you a feeling you really like is one of the reasons why you and everyone else goes there. You can do this with your own space.

Lighting

Have you ever actually thought much about lighting? If you haven't then you are really missing a trick. Very simply, a floor lamp/desk lamp or two with not too bright bulbs means the lighting is right, not too much, not too little. Put them in different corners so the light is diffused across the room and this really is all you need.

You don't want your room light on, way too much brightness and doesn't give the room any feel of possibility or cool. A very simple fix. Buy a candle you like the smell of. Might not sound like something you might normally do, but it will make a big difference.

Music

You might or might not want music playing. Sometimes you just want the sound of breathing and this is completely cool. Some people get a bit freaked out by the intimacy of silence and breathing. It can be a little intense sometimes, but when you are completely into someone it is just another layer to sharing intimacy with them. Sharing silence, hearing each other's changing breathing as things hot up, this is very, very cool.

However, If you want to play tunes while you are getting it on, then choose something you like, but not something you are likely to be singing along to in your head. Your focus is on your partner, not on some band you are particularly into right now.

This is obviously a very personal choice and will require some experimentation on your part. Do be prepared for your partner to be asking 'What is this music? Is this your hot sex playlist?' If she does say this and has a bit of a giggle at your expense because she doesn't like it then I suggest you tell her it is your hot sex playlist and if she has anything to contribute she is very welcome to add to it. After all, you both do need to be enjoying the environment.

The best way to start is to experiment with a range of styles. After all you aren't going to feel like the same playlist every time. So maybe you put an indie band-led playlist together, get an ultra-cool downtempo beat-based list, a super cool laid back list, an up tempo groove with more funk and faster beats, an uptempo and downtempo R&B selection and finally maybe an orchestral mood selection for very late night, super slow sessions. Each one of these playlists should have a good hour worth of tunes, so at least 25 different songs.

Having a range of already prepared tunes as an old-school mix-tape style offer means your environment is already prepared and you don't have to think about tunes when you want to be thinking about her. Also, if she isn't sure about your ultra-cool downtempo beats, then you can immediately switch to something more to her liking.

Putting these playlists together is a fun thing to do, and in particular putting these playlists together with your partner, then road-testing their atmospheric qualities, is an excellent thing to do.

There are playlists online that other people have compiled that are a good place to start if you are stuck for a beginning. They will also give you an introduction to a world of music you might have no idea about, and in the process giving you bragging rights to knowing cool artists no-one else will know.

65

All the things to consider

The Details..

Now you have your atmosphere right, your lighting right, your music sorted etc….. It is down to getting on with having an incredible time with your partner. There are elements here we need to talk about that you might or might not know about, but will help with everything you do. They range from the wider picture to the smallest gesture.

Layering the touch you give

Remember, going straight into penetrative sex without fore-play and without leading your partner into a 'pleasure zone' is not what we want to do.

Foreplay is about leading you and your partner into more and more responsive sensations. And foreplay is about layering these sensations in different ways, in different places on the body. To do this you need to begin to learn how to know what is happening to her.

Awareness and sensitivity to your partner/paying attention and properly noticing your partner

How you develop sensitivity and awareness of how your partner responds to your actions is crucial to your development as a skilled and knowledgeable partner. The following areas are the most important to be focusing on to build your skills.

These areas are:

1. Her Breathing
2. Changes in skin
3. Response to touch

To get an understanding of what is happening to your partner as your intimacy session develops, you are going to have to be aware of how these different areas of change actually happen. How much you notice and how much you pay attention to change is going to determine how successful you are at doing this.

Change in breathing

First of all notice in yourself your own change in breathing when you are getting aroused. Do you breathe faster? Slower? Do you take deeper breaths? So how do you witness these changes in your partner? Can you feel her breathing change through your touch? Can you feel her muscles unwinding and softening? Is the time for inbreath and then outbreath longer?

Changes in skin.

Awareness of skin changes is a subtle one, and one that takes practice along with gaining touch sensitivity. Her process of arousal will increase blood flow around her body, meaning her skin will become warmer and you might find an increased 'tautness' to her skin as well, as the tissue below the surface becomes filled with blood.

This increased blood flow is also linked to an increased sensitivity to those areas she finds arousing. So when she is getting aroused her clitoris becomes full of blood, not unlike you getting wood. However, focus on these areas when at early stages of arousal is generally not going to be helpful, as the blood and responsive nerve endings just won't react to your efforts, and you might just make the area sore. Part of the practice here is getting to know when certain areas become responsive, and gently stroking and engaging them at that moment. And part of this is being patient and waiting until the time is right. And make sure you use lube. Lots of it.

Sometimes her arousal will be super quick, like when you go from not hard to almost exploding hard in what seems like 2 seconds. The more you understand what is happening to her, the better your response to it will be.

Touch

The skin is the largest organ in the human body. It is home to millions of nerve receptors and is capable of giving hugely varying sensitivity, from the almost numb to the jump out of your chair at the lightest brush. So the way you touch someone's skin has serious consequences for the way they react. .

Touching, stroking, pinching, applying pressure to and having the lightest of touches on skin, and then knowing when and how each of these different approaches to contact can have the maximum effect, is one of the great secrets of amazing lovemaking. Do you know how to do all these variations and everything in between?

Do you know when to apply these variations and then how to layer them to get your partner to a peak of pleasure? And do you have the awareness and sensitivity in your hands, your palms and especially your fingers to ensure you can work with a serious range of pressure?

When you realise she isn't into what you are doing.

Reiterating what is one of the major points of this book, you will also be able to see very clearly when your partner just isn't into what you are doing. And when you notice this, it is absolutely your responsibility to stop. If her breathing is clearly demonstrating discomfort, not happy, not enjoying herself, then stop. You will be the bigger man for noticing before she says anything.

If you wait until she asks you to stop then she will have possibly been uncomfortable for a while. And it might be she doesn't ask you to stop, just gets it over with as quickly as possible, because part of this cultural narrative is a) she doesn't want to upset you by asking you to stop because you might not like her anymore, b) she is worried you might get angry and maybe physically aggressive, c) she thinks you think you have a right to keep going because you have a rod on (believe me, people believe this), and again, this triggers a fear of a violent reprisal.

There are countless accounts online of this kind of thing happening. She isn't into what her partner is doing, he thinks he is being the king of the bedroom and she is having an amazing time so she decides it is easier to keep going and put up with not having a nice time because due to her past experience,the idea of stopping him at this point could be dangerous, difficult or unpleasant. Don't let this happen to you. Be tuned in.

If she isn't into it, and because of your super ninja powers of noticing you become clearly aware of it, then stop. Maybe she just needs you to change what you are doing, where you are touching, the speed, the pressure.

Maybe she just fell out of the feeling of wanting to be intimate and just isn't feeling like she wants to continue. The reason she wants to stop is irrelevant. She wants to stop. You stop. You can jerk off later. Your first concern is to make sure she is OK. And You Have To Stop.

Sensitivity and areas of focus

When working through the processes of touching and stroking your partner there are a number of areas you can explore that you might not know will have a fantastic impact. if you have never spent time exploring the skin and possibilities this will unleash, it may be she also doesn't know the impact either so maybe you can explore together.

Before we start talking about this though a reminder of context and in particular, let's talk about over-stimulation and too-much-too-soon.

If in the process of exploring intimacy she isn't ready for significant physical intensity from your touch, then she will be turned off by the experience. And that may well be the end of the session.

The significant intensity can come from two basic processes. One is you are just going too fast and with too much intensity for it to feel good. The second is where you are trying to do too many things and she is overwhelmed by all the information her nervous system is telling her.

So when exploring these different possibilities with your partner, start gently and start with low intensity. Also go steady and be consistent with what you are doing. Consistency of movement is very important. Finally, remember that what worked yesterday might not work today. So keep an open mind about what you do and how she responds.

Areas of the body

Let's talk first about the areas of the body that aren't genital or breast focused. So essentially the rest of the body. And I'm not going to get into anything fetish-like here either.

Let's break this into two groups.

1. The obvious ones
2. The not very obvious ones.

Keep in mind everyone is different. For example, some people love their neck being kissed, others can't bear it. What worked on someone else as a site for great exploration and sensation may be a complete turnoff for the person you are with.

The obvious ones

These are areas known and loved the world over as erogenous zones that can be mined forever and, depending on your partner's mind state, one of these is very likely to yield positive responses.

These include:

1. The neck
2. The ears including the ear lobes
3. The sides of the hips
4. The inside of the thighs

The reality is there is huge variation across each of these areas as well.

The Neck:

When talking about the neck as an area of sensitivity, I am talking about the side of the neck. There is a broad range of sensitivity from the base of the neck, essentially the top of the shoulders, to where the neck meets the jaw. The sensitivity of the neck generally increases the higher you go, so if you are stroking then kissing here, I would suggest you start low and work up toward the jaw.

Stroking gently is good for the neck, but really kissing is the best way to engage with what the neck offers you.

You can however, if you are kissing the neck, find your other hand to the back of her neck and stroke gently there at the same time. This kind of *double sensation* is ultimately what you want to have happen as often as possible. You want two separate sensations complementing one another to provide an experience that is more than the individual ones by themselves. Also be aware you have to measure out the intensity of each of these movements. One needs to be more intense than the other, because if both are full-on experiences in themselves and you do it too early, it will be too much.

There are a variety of ways any stroking can happen, so let's explore the stroking of the back of the neck as an example of what could be done.

The best way to stroke the back of the neck is from the base of the skull down to the top of the shoulders, and this could be done with either the full palm sliding down, the fingers working gently like you are softly going through the motions of playing a piano as you slide down from the skull, one or two fingers working at the same time and rather than your fingers sliding it could be your nails making contact, with a very light scratching sensation that can feel so so good.

This double action requires some coordination skills to pull off successfully, and there are ways you can train yourself to do this better in the next section. There is a lot you can play with to ensure skin contact is maximised, but not overwhelming. Remember, stimulation is a game of balance, and the joy of it is the playing of that balance.

The ears (especially the earlobes)

As potentially a target for advancing up your partner's neck is the ear, especially the earlobe. As with everything, your partner's sensitivity to attention here will be unique, and will change on a daily basis. Remember, some will love this and others will hate it.

The ear is super sensitive, so go carefully. Gently sucking on the earlobe can feel amazing, but there are some who find it creepy. Gently nibbling on the earlobe can have the same response.

Something to be particularly careful of is sticking your tongue in her ear. There is something akin to being licked to death by your dog rendering this action a rather significant arousal destroyer. Maybe she might like it? Then play around with when she likes it. But really, there are more interesting things to do with your tongue.

The sides of the hips

The sides of the hips are an area of the body that can also be engaged with clothes on as much as clothes off. And this is especially true if you are in a casual situation, sitting watching TV, or just talking in close proximity with each other, maybe having a quiet and quick kiss during the day or in the evening, and sometimes some ninja hip stroking is awesome when you are out and about, in a crowded place, kiss her and just spend a lingering moment with a hand stroking her hip. If there is an opportunity to touch/stroke your partner, then the side of the hip is an excellent place to choose.

Stroking the side of the hip while talking, in a non-suggestive, non-sexual way will be an opportunity for you to make her feel good through the contact with your hand, and to make you feel good through being able to have contact and be with her. There is something about a hand on the hip that is greater than you might think. There is something about it that anchors both of you. Something to play with.

Stroking the side of the hips when in an intimate session also brings great rewards, especially if you are able to explore a lot of variation with pressure, with gentle squeezing, and with differing exploration through use of your palm through to your fingers.

So, again paying attention to her level of arousal begin to explore variations of pressure. Also making sure no change is too quick and likely to bring her out of the pleasure she is in, begin to move from light to pressured.

Pushing on the front of the hips

While you are in the flow of intimacy and you are inside your partner, sometimes you can push down on her hip joint, gently pushing down as you push deeper inside her. If this is too heavy handed, it won't work as you wish and will be painful and uncomfortable but sometimes you can time the push down with a gentle thrust and she will be very happy you have done so.

This is something to play with in small increments. You can start with a push on the hips before any of the more serious action happens. To do so use the palm of your hand, so your right hand to her left hip, and get the front of her hip into the middle of the palm of your hand, then spread the rest of your palm across her skin as you apply a little pressure. Try various pressures. Sometimes just the contact is all you need. Like you are holding all of her in the palm of your hand. Sometimes a lot of pressure feels amazing. You will have to judge this yourself.

The inside thighs

The inside thighs are a very obvious and sensitive area to be working with, stroking, applying pressure and just generally giving attention to. The challenge I have for you with paying attention to the inside thighs is for you to do it when you aren't thinking about following up with any intimate contact.

The inside thighs can often be a gateway point before the heavier fun begins, so often the impact a considered and focused period of time stroking the inner thigh can bring is not experienced as there is too much anticipation of what happens next. Take your time.

Also be careful as the inside thighs can also be very ticklish, so a very light touch might do the opposite and result in your hand being swatted away as your touch tickles.

Try this when your partner still has underwear on, so while you may get to a point where the pants come off, you are focused on the actions of stroking the thighs as the end point themselves, rather than being distracted by the possibilities that beckons between them.

The not very obvious places

There are some fantastic and not very obvious places where pleasure is to be found. I am sure you have all found your partner's particular places, and you are aware of how these change as your intimacy evolves.

The base of the spine / lumbar to sacrum

The area of the lower back to where the spine meets the pelvis and then directly below that meeting point, so the lumbar spine area then onto the sacrum is a super sensitive and deeply pleasurable place to place your attention. And this area reaps great rewards no matter what state of arousal your partner is in.

There are a range of options with the base of the spine, and you need to try them all at some point, but start with just placing your hand here when kissing or hugging, particularly when you have your clothes on. And you can place your hand here and either have a light touch, or place your hand here and apply a little bit of pressure. This pressure can mean you are pushing her slightly into you, which then brings the front of the both of you together with a little more pressure in the contact.

When you are a little further into your intimate session, and by now may or may not have clothes on, when kissing or stroking her you might start to apply small pressure like a gentle massage to this area.

This area is amazing to explore in the middle of sex, while you are getting your tongue involved, or when you are inside her.

The Entirety of her Back

The whole of her back is a wonderful erogenous zone that responds astoundingly well to gentle stroking or if the feeling is right, to a little more pressure on the skin.

You might stroke her back as you are kissing her, just stroke her back if she is lying on her front as an exploration of her body, maybe a gentle massage of her shoulders leading into stroking down her body or in the throes of passion, particularly if you are taking her from behind, gentle pressure on her skin and into her back muscles can elevate her experience.

Back of her knees and inside her elbows

These are quite surprising to most people, but the reality is, with the right amount of pressure both of these places can reward attention. The feeling here isn't one of blow-your-mind pleasure, but more of an additional pleasurable feeling added to other actions. Stroking the back of the knee is, however, quite a specific action probably happening when you are either solely focused on just this or are enjoying working down your partner's legs. Inside the elbow is more amenable to being part of a double process where you are touching 2 different places at once.

Final note

A final note here is if you are watching porn for your sexual tips, you will not see anyone doing any of this. Porn is fixated on cock and pussy. In this book we are fixated on the whole body and in particular how we can create multiple sensations for our partner. In porn, they are looking to get as much footage of penetration, mouth, arse or pussy, as possible. So don't expect to see anything you have read about so far illustrated in a porn clip you are watching.

66

Your intimate session

67

Step by Step

Beginning your intimate session

The beginning of your intimate encounter can start in a multitude of ways, and rarely will it happen the same way twice. For beginners in the world of intimate relations, and for dickhead blokes who think only of their cock and nothing else, nothing is interesting or has happened until the girlfriend is either riding or sucking his cock. And the outcome here is he shoots his load in 2 to 3 minutes, if he can stay that long, thinking the sex was awesome and she is left thinking 'why am I here and why am I wasting my time. He's a dickhead'.

Your encounter and the feeling of intense intimacy that comes with it doesn't start when you get undressed. Remember, girls are interested in exploring their sexuality and pleasure as much as you are. You might have been thinking about this for days or weeks. It is likely so has she. You might have been fantasizing about this moment for months, and it is likely so has she. So if you have time together beforehand, then use the time to build the feeling between you.

You might have spent all day with your sexual partner, but not in a sexual way. You might have been hanging out together, doing things together. Totally non-sexual. But the prospect of what might happen later is going to be in the air between you. There will be tension, good tension, and expectation. You might have had to excuse yourself a couple of times because you got yourself a boner just thinking about it and don't want to embarrass yourself in public. It has happened to all of us, so don't let it embarrass you.

This time spent before you get intimate is a really important opportunity to start physical contact. Just light touch. It might be that you kiss her a little more frequently than normal and your hands are resting on her hips or her back with a touch more pressure than normal. Maybe when you are talking with her you hold her hand, or you just have contact.

While you are exploring this, remember: Don't be weird and creepy. So what I am not saying is throughout the day pin her down and stick your tongue down her throat. Don't grab her on the hips and start dry humping her and say 'this is what you're getting later'. Believe me, some guys think this is sexy and she wants it. Maybe this is true, but in conversations and reading about these situations, it is unlikely. You don't even need to go this far for you to blow it. If you do too much and it is out of character, then she will be getting creeped out because it will feel like she is with someone else. Go gently and judge the mood.

The longer term impacts of having extra touch when doing normal or mundane things is that it will become part of your relationship, and this extra contact then has implications for when you are getting intimate. And ultimately, if you are with someone and you have this contact and share this with someone all the time, the entire relationship becomes one where both of you are feeling physical pleasure all the time you are together, and with clothes on as much as clothes off.

Remember though, if she doesn't like extra contact and she says to back off, you know what to do. Exactly as she wants. The point here is your intimate encounter can last for 12 hours, and it is only the last hour which is the one where you are naked and having sex. The feeling of touch and pleasure of being in contact with each other and of being the object of gentle but intense attention significantly improves the final naked lust.

Beginning to get your clothes off.

So now you have reached the point where you are alone with your partner and you are starting to get hotter with each other, kissing, touching, stroking her skin, getting your clothes off one by one.

This is another opportunity for an amateur to make a mistake. Getting so excited that you just go for pussy with your hands. Calm down and take a little more time.

Remember, if you start to pick the pace up, get super excited and fast with your actions, it is unlikely you are going to last very long. And what we want to be able to do is last for as long as we can. Elsewhere in the book we talk about not worrying if you come too quickly, so this might seem to be a contradiction. It isn't. Sometimes you will just lose your mind in passion and you will be done very quickly, other times you might last hours and not actually ejaculate at all. What we are trying to do here is set yourself up so you can last as long as possible.

So calm down. You might want to stroke her skin for longer,

kiss her for longer. It might be that she has just gone for your cock and is doing everything under the sun to blow your little mind. Of course, you aren't going to stop her. But remember, your focus is on her pleasure, so keep that in mind as she is focusing on you.

And keep in mind, every time you do this it will be different from every other time. Even if it is the same time every day for a month, it will be different as you will be different. And sometimes you will dive into hands and tongues in from the get-go. Other times it might take you an hour to get there, or you might not ever get there at all. Be open to being in the moment and the more exploration you do and the more aware of what is going on you become, the better you will be at judging the moment.

Beginning and about to move on to the next level

So you have begun to get intimate with your partner, kissing, stroking her skin, whatever you do to start yourselves off. You are in a position where you think your partner is ready for some extra stimulation from you and you make your decision to get your hands involved.

In the first instance, this is where you might apply lubricant of your own to ensure smooth running of the proceedings. To start with this could just be a little bit of spit on your fingers (if you have excellent hygiene) or take a moment to apply lubricant to your fingers instead. I think sometimes there might be a concern that you have got into the swing of things and don't want to interrupt the momentum by pausing for 20 seconds to get lubricant on your fingers. Don't worry about the interruption. Better to pause for 20 seconds to create extraordinary pleasure. She will be happy for the extra stimulation and fun it brings.

8000 nerve endings

Now we are about to get our hands involved, you need to know all about the Clitoris. Check out the diagram below. First bit of information you need to know is that the head of the clitoris has 8000 nerve endings, which is a hell of a lot of sensitivity. Considering the end of your cock has less than half of this number, you get an idea of what the response to the right kind of stimulation might be. And you might also get an idea of the feeling of the wrong kind of stimulation might be as well.

If you are new to the discovery of the clitoris, the advice is to go slow, go gently and go softly. Here is the image of the female genital anatomy to remind you where you are going.

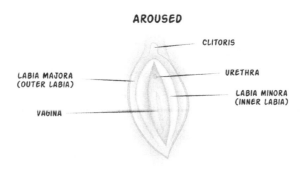

Vulva

(On a side note, you might have watched porn where a lot of the clitoral stimulation when an individual is stimulating another involves smacking and hitting the clitoris. Unless this is specifically asked for, don't.)

Alongside not smacking and hitting the clitoris, it also isn't a game console control. 8000 nerve endings = incredibly sensitive. Go gently.

Some important information about the clitoris

There has been a great deal of focus on the importance of oral sex for men to ensure their partner is going to have a good time. And I don't disagree. In the great variety of ways to please your lover, there are very few better ways of getting your partner to orgasm than getting your tongue and mouth involved.

But the challenge with a lot of this focus is the idea that oral sex is the only way this can happen. This is blatantly untrue and suggests a lack of experimentation and desire on the part of the authors of these ideas to get their hands and fingers going and trying new and wonderful things.

THE STRUCTURE OF THE CLITORIS

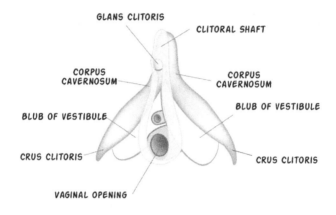

GLANS CLITORIS

CLITORAL SHAFT

CORPUS CAVERNOSUM

CORPUS CAVERNOSUM

BLUB OF VESTIBULE

BLUB OF VESTIBULE

CRUS CLITORIS

CRUS CLITORIS

VAGINAL OPENING

'I can't find it (you) / He can't find it(your partner)'

Let's talk about the classic line 'I can't find it(you) / He can't find it(your partner)'. A classic line to diminish the perceived prowess of the male partner, and a classic line from blokes who genuinely struggle in their intimate relations to find and work this extraordinary part of the body.

I have also heard from blokes that they don't need to find it because this is what a cock is for. What I don't understand is why a little bit of gentle and kind instruction from your partner doesn't occur around the stroking and attention to the clitoris. It would certainly benefit both partners in a range of ways but perhaps it comes down to not knowing how to have those conversations.

And let's be honest here, yes, the glans of the clitoris can be a little challenging to find if you are fumbling about and not particularly interested in finding it and having a play. Check out the diagram above. But if you are serious about creating the conditions for ultimate pleasure for your partner you have to take your time and explore. And ask your partner for help and instruction if you realise she isn't quite feeling it. And maybe a demonstration of what feels the best.

If your partner is aroused, then the clitoris is already engorged with blood and shouldn't be hard to find. If it is still very difficult to find then you probably need to do more to arouse your partner. The hard and erect clitoris is a marvel to behold.

The reality is everyone's anatomy is different, sometimes the hood of skin covering the clitoris covers it more than others and in others the clitoris is quite exposed all the time.

Every body is different and every clitoris is different. Some are long, some are short. The base of some are close to the surface of the body, others are quite deep. Some have hoods completely covering them, others don't. Clitoris size and shape is like cock size and shape. Everyone is different and unique. Enjoy the process of exploring uniqueness.

Contact

The first moment of contact with her most sensitive areas is so very important.

This moment of first contact is exquisite and profound, every time you do it. You might have had sex with this person hundreds of times, but it doesn't lessen the power of this moment. And how you make this touch will give her enormous amounts of information about you, where you are at with her pleasure and how you might be intending on taking things forward. If you are rushed, and just swamp her with fumbling hands and getting your fingers inside and pumping hard, it just isn't going to be fun and she may well just stop you there and then. I hope she will.

But if your touch is gentle, firm and knowing but not heavy, and she feels you exploring in interesting and sensitive ways, the information she is getting is you are there for her pleasure and you are wanting to find the ways you can give her an incredible time. This information is crucial to her being in the state of receiving attention and then flying into a pleasure orbit.

It is also important to remember that the body is changing and evolving all the time. How she is today is not how she was yesterday and not how she will be tomorrow. This will impact how relaxed she is, how into you she is and how into the moment she is and this will impact her lubrication and her sensitivity. Everything you do and experience will be different every time you have sex.

So get used to engaging with this process of care and respect when you first make contact. There are two distinct choices to make here about applying the first lot of lubricant.

Before you apply, be aware of the temperature of it. A lot of lubricants are cold, and while for some the application of cold items on hot skin is an extra turn-on, think ice on the skin, at this early stage of proceedings you have to be careful that applying cold lubricant to her most delicate of areas is potentially going to snap her out of whatever state you have so carefully and expertly found together.

A simple solution. Warm it up. Maybe sitting the container in a bowl of warm water. If you are in Autumn or Winter and the heating is on, sit the lubricant on a radiator to warm up. If neither of those is possible, put some on your fingers and warm it up. Remember if you warm the container up, it will be runnier when it comes out. There is nothing quite like warm lubricant running quickly out of a container when you don't expect it. It goes everywhere.

There are two choices to make here about applying the first lot of lubricant.

1. Gently apply the lubricant to the top of her vagina, directly on the clitoris, and not any further down.
2. Gently apply the lubricant you are using to the top of her vagina and gently continue the application downward so you are able to cover most of her.

For the first choice you are choosing to spend some time focused solely on her clitoris and for the second choice, you are preparing for a couple of ways of stimulating her.

Clitoral focus

There are so many possibilities and so many different choices you can make about how you begin to stimulate your partner. I repeat: softly, gently and carefully are all very important beginning points.

As you apply the lubricant, be aware of how you are applying it. Are you applying then rubbing it on with a bit of friction? Are you applying then stroking up and down? Are you stroking side to side? Are you making circles on her? And what is she doing in response to your attention?

However you begin, you should be listening for changes of breathing, feeling for hip movements as she positively responds to you as you are touching her and for any other signs you know means she is enjoying the attention.

So you have applied lubricant and you are moving your fingers in varying ways across the exposed part of her clitoris. There is something else you can begin to explore here. Take her clitoris in between your finger and thumb and gently squeeze. This will be slippery due to the lubricant on it, but if you slip off you shouldn't be squeezing so hard that it won't feel abrupt and a bit weird.

So once you have squeezed a couple of times and have got your pressure right try squeezing and then rolling the clitoris between your finger and thumb a couple of times. This obviously distributes pressure around the area.

And once you have tried rolling between your fingers, now see if you can start at the base, then roll and slide your fingers up and off in one long stroke. So we are essentially trying to get as much stimulation along the most of the clitoris as possible, remember those 8000 nerve endings? So if we gently grip and squeeze, then roll and stroke to the top of her, we have a big chance of engaging a lot of those nerve ends.

If you are exploring this little technique you might want to begin to apply a little pressure to the very base of her clitoris, where the visible and tangible part attaches to the rest of the organ, the part that sits relatively deeply under the skin. In the meantime, you might want to begin engaging this section by adding a little pressure as you are squeezing and stroking. So now you have this little technique sorted out, alternate a little.

Go back to stroking, either up or down or side to side. Vary your speed a little and vary your pressure. Go extremely light so there is almost no contact, then slowly apply pressure so you feel like you are getting a good grip, then loosen off again.

Notice what is happening with her. Obviously you want to see what the impact is of this attention, so you need to be noticing how her breathing is changing, how her skin is changing, what sort of pressure she is putting into your hand, and keep working with the techniques

Different techniques

There are a lot of different ways of effectively stroking the clitoris. Remember, while what you might have done previously was brilliant, it doesn't mean it is going to work the same today, so you have to have variations in what you are doing. If what worked a treat last session isn't working this session, you have changes you can immediately make that are very likely to help you. With this in mind there are three variations in your action you want to be playing with to ensure a range of possibilities.

These are:

Change the direction of your contact.

Instead of continuing vertically, up and down, you try side to side instead. Instead of having straight lines of action you play with circles. Those circles can then go from clockwise to counterclockwise. You can get very fancy and track figures of 8 across the clitoris then explore the grip and stroke ideas above.

And you can combine these and mix them up, but tread

carefully. A consistent angle of stimulation that is predictable and working is much more desirable than you trying to vary everything at super speed. Which brings me to the next variation

Speed

Variations on speed are obvious, and the more into it you both are the more likely you are to go fast.

A caution here with regard to speed. If you are getting carried away and start kicking into overdrive and going fast, and she isn't ready for that kind of intensity, it is going to have the opposite effect and be a very rapid turnoff for her.

So keep your action relatively slow, and even when you are tempted to speed up a lot, don't, unless of course she is asking you to. Then you do what you're asked. But if she is enjoying what you are doing, don't change it. Finally, the last variation to talk through is

Pressure.

I think this is the most useful variation to play with, but also the hardest as you will need to have achieved a certain level of sensitivity with your touch to ensure you are delivering what you think you are delivering.

The extremes of pressure can both have essentially the same impact, in that both can be extraordinarily pleasurable and both can also be really annoying and wrong to do.

The reality is that a super light touch can have a profound impact on your partner, so don't underestimate what is possible when you are lightly stroking her.. There is also something non-confrontational and non-challenging about a soft light touch. There is something nurturing, gentle and supportive about it, and if you show or are clear by your actions you are very happy to work softly and gently with her for as long as she needs it, then this is the perfect place for you to start.

However, some people won't like a very light touch and will need a clear feeling of pressure and contact. Again, you have to be sensitive to your situation and how she is responding.

Continuing on……

Now you have lubricated her and your fingers (your lube is obviously warm) and you start by making light circles on her clitoris, playing with different amounts of pressure, finding out what she likes.

You change to vertical strokes with a bit more pressure, with the start of your movement beginning to contact the skin at the base of her clit to begin to make contact with the rest of the organ under her skin.

After some time spent exploring here you decide to grip her between your thumb and index finger and gently squeeze. You then roll her between your fingers as you draw your fingers from the base to the tip.

Next

By this stage, if you have been reading her responses and developing what you are doing based on these, she should be in a perfectly pleasurable state, with a smile on her face and excited by what might be happening next.

So in response to your perfectly stroked attention she might be moist (but remember, that isn't necessarily the case) but also the lube you applied earlier should also have traveled down her labia. If you are in a position where you think you could do with some more lubricant, apply some more.

Now you are going to travel your fingers from her clitoris, down between the lips of her labia to the entrance to her vagina..

Back to actions

You have stroked your partner in a range of ways, have got her feeling amazing, have traveled your finger down her and are about to enter her. With plenty more lubricant, you slowly and gently enter her. With this slow and gentle consideration, it is very helpful to your action that as you get deeper, you start to make circles with your finger, trying to touch the vaginal walls as you go. This is to help spread the lubricant, but also to open her vagina a little.

With all of the above, remember, your starting action is slowly, carefully and sensitively. Your partner might be saying to you that she wants you to go harder, to stroke her with more pressure, to get your fingers inside her sooner. If this is what she wants, then do it. Follow her requests, help her fly.

The point of starting slowly and gently is that it is the best way to start. You can go faster and with more pressure from here. But if you start with pressure and speed, it can and will be a big turnoff.

Remember also that the hard and fast pumping action with two fingers jabbing in and out of her that you might see in porn really isn't a reality of what gets people off. It isn't fun. It really doesn't have that much of an impact in any way and is really quite aggressive. Again though, if that is what she wants you to do as it gives her exquisite and maximum pleasure, then get in there. Sometimes that hard and fast movement is with the internal fingers applying pressure to the top of the inside wall, and that can be amazing. This isn't what I am talking about.

I have read numerous times on forums of women talking about their partners just jabbing their fingers in and out of their vaginas. They are perplexed, very annoyed, very disappointed and confused as to what is going on, as there is no contact in this action with any sensitive part of their anatomy, and the jabbing action has no intimacy and no care.

Don't do this.

Two areas that are worth spending time with. The G-Spot.

I am sure you have heard about, been told about or have read about the famous G-spot. This is an area that is on the upper wall of the vagina, around 2-3 centimetres in, and is found by the fact that it has a slightly different texture of skin. The skin feels slightly 'ribbed' and slightly stronger. If you have been doing the finger sensitivity exercises that are in the appendix you will be able to feel this easily.

There are a bunch of ideas about what the g-spot actually is, but that doesn't really matter to us. We just need to know that paying attention to this area, whatever it might be, has a very positive impact on your partner's pleasure.

Back to the plan

You have got your fingers involved and have found the g-spot. Again, starting gently and softly, start to stimulate this area with your finger, starting with light pressure and doing similar movements to those you did earlier, up and down, side to side, circles and any range of different variations of these.

As you spend more time here, start to apply more pressure as your finger moves back and forth. A similar story as before, you should be adjusting your speed and pressure depending on how she is responding to your attentions. While you are applying more pressure through the pad of your finger and giving her the attention she needs, be aware that the rest of your finger can also be useful.

There is often just attention on what the pad of your finger is doing to the g-spot, but considering the majority of the body of the clitoris surrounds the entrance to the vagina, you will want your actions to also mean your rest of your finger is in contact with the wall close to the entrance.

And lastly in this position, if you are in the right angle for it, align the palm of your hand with the top of the clitoris and apply gentle pressure. This means that as the end of your finger is stroking the g-spot and the base of your finger is touching the inner walls, the base of the palm of your hand is gently in contact with and rubbing the top of the clitoris that you have so perfectly engaged and stimulated previously.

Be careful with how much pressure you use with the palm of your hand here, as it is quite a blunt instrument and you don't want all your previous handy work to suddenly be reversed because you are thudding your palm into one of your partner's most sensitive areas, and particularly as you have stimulated it to be super sensitive already.

However, if you are able to create a gentle pressure in your hand that works, you will be stimulating her in 3 different ways.

2nd focal point

The second point that is worth spending time on and working in a similar way to the g-spot is almost on the opposite side, and this is an area on the base of the vaginal wall. This is much easier to engage when you are going down on her but is something to think about when you are just getting your fingers involved as well.

To find this spot you are to insert your finger inside your partner but rather than palm up like you are going to be working her g-spot you have your palm down and you stimulate the skin at the base of the entrance to her vagina. There is a similar length of skin to work on as the g-spot, and a slightly different feeling of the tissue, similar to the g-spot, but not as pronounced. Work similarly to what we have already discussed, so start with gentle stroking and build the pressure and speed as you go. If you haven't tried this before and you're not sure what you are doing, start by alternating between stimulating the g-spot for a short while, then move your position here for a short while and then move back to the g-spot.

This may be extremely annoying to your partner, as she could be kicking into a very pleasurable thing from your g-spot manipulation and then you go and change your point of stimulation and her pleasure adventure is halted. So be aware if this is indeed the case and by changing position you are screwing things up. It is very possible so again you have to be aware and adjust what you are doing as you go.

Joining it all together.

So now your job is to join the technique of stimulating her clitoris and g-spot at the same time, and not with the same hand as described above, but with each hand giving attention to its own area.

You can do this while lying down, although it can be a bit challenging in terms of how you negotiate the position of her body while you make it work. It could turn into one of those comedic sex moments where you are trying to do something interesting and it just turns into a stupid idea but is worth a laugh and a giggle. At least you are trying something new.

The best way is to be sat up next to her, or on your knees, whatever position means you are both comfortable. And you will need to be comfortable because once you start this, she isn't going to want you to stop.

So if she is lying on her back, you need to be seated next to her hips so that you don't have to bend too far forward to get both hands on her.

I suggest that you work in this way after you have already achieved success with the attention you have given her with your hands, and that you have already been working her g-spot and she is seriously aroused. She may even by this time have had a couple of orgasms due to your attention.

If she hasn't that is fine as well. Don't begin judging yourself on whether she has orgasmed within the first 10 minutes of touching her. Sometimes she will and sometimes she won't. This is again one of the glorious delights of being in the moment and responding to how she is responding to your attention.

You might think that you have been working her like a total sex god, technique perfect, sensitivity in your fingers amazing, your touch on fire and responding to her like the perfect partner and she just isn't feeling it. Another time you might be a bit half-arsed about what you're doing and she is exploding like firecrackers….. You just don't know what is going to happen, so as long as you are committed, gentle, use loads of lube and start slowly, everything will work out.)

So you are sitting beside her, she is hot and aroused and feeling sexy and loving the attention you are giving her. You will need to refresh your lubricant situation, so get more on both fingers and make sure it is warm.

If you are sitting on her right side, then you might like to stimulate her clitoris with your right hand before moving into her and using your right fingers on her g-spot and swapping clitoral stimulation to your left hand.

(This is really the primary reason why all of the sensitivity and strength exercises that are in the appendix are for both hands. If you only work with one hand, then when you come to pleasure her with both hands, it will be clear that you are fumbling when your non-dominant hand doesn't have the sensitivity or skill in touching her. You need to be developing an ambidextrous skill set when it comes to this work.)

So you now have your right fingers stimulating her g-spot and your left fingers working her clitoris. Considering she is already aroused, begin with a little more pressure in both areas than you previously started with. Make sure with your left hand that you are consistent with what you are doing.

Another consideration here is that while she is already aroused, the intensity of this kind of stimulation can be overwhelming if you try to go too fast too quickly. And obviously the last thing we want is for the feelings to be suddenly so intense that it pulls her out of her state and turns her off because it is too much to deal with. So again, this is about working your way up to intensity, and following her lead in giving her more pressure and speed as she wants to experience it.

This kind of attention, with confident and clear movements at the centre of all your actions, is very likely to bring her to one or several orgasms. If you see that she is moving toward having an epic experience, don't change what you are doing. Sometimes you will be tempted to speed up, you will get caught up in the moment and you will automatically start to increase intensity. This can throw her off her stride and again, pull her out of her state, so you don't want this to happen.

She is close to orgasm because what you are doing is working, so don't change that. Keep it consistent and the journey she is on will take her to where she wants to go. And you will be tempted, and it is hard to resist, but you must.... And the only reason you might speed up at this point is if that is what she asks you to do. And as with everything in this book, if she asks you to do it, then do it.

68

There is a lot of information here. Don't be alarmed.

Before we move on to the next level, I want to make sure you aren't alarmed by the amount of information so far. You don't need to 'do' all these things. They are options and ideas. The reality is that if you are curious and have a desire to bring magical pleasure to your partner, you are already most of the way towards being amazing in bed. The techniques and ideas you have just read about really are the beginning of your journey, but they give you an idea of where and how to start.

Don't panic, breathe deeply. All will be good.

69

Moving On

Going down

One of your next options in terms of bringing your partner exquisite pleasure is giving her oral sex or going down on her. You will remember earlier the 3 elements that most women said were responsible for orgasms? Going down was one of them.

Performing oral sex on your partner and doing it well will bring her to the next level of orgasms, as you will be able to stimulate her clitoris with your tongue and lips, and then use one of your hands to stroke her g-spots while using your other hand to continue to stimulate her skin. This multi-stimulating approach pays epic dividends in the land of epic orgasms.

First things first. Oral sex is glorious and fun. The first time you adventure into wrapping your mouth around your partner's most intimate areas, you will notice that there is a particular scent to her that you won't have noticed before. This isn't a bad scent, this is an exquisite scent and, if you have been doing all that has been described earlier, you will be mostly responsible for this as her normal vaginal secretions will be mixed with more lubricant from her orgasms.

Body position

When you are moving into position to go down on your partner, be aware of where the rest of your body is. You might approach her from the side, but that will mean your body weight will be heavily on one of her legs, which might go numb. This might be a distraction for her, so be aware of this. We don't want distractions.

If you are between her legs, ensure you aren't lying on her leg or foot in any way, for the reasons just stated. Another position is that she might be straddling your face, in which case she just has to make sure she is comfortable and you have to ensure that you can breathe.

One last thing before we get into details. If you have a coarse face stubble from not shaving for a day or two, then have a shave before a session. Scraping a stubbly beard across your most intimate parts, well, just image someone rubbing sandpaper across the end of your knob. Get it? Enjoyable? Didn't think so.

There are a wide range of actions that are open to you when you go down on your partner. We won't discuss all of them here but will focus on a couple that you can explore in more detail at your, and your partner's, leisure.

We will focus on two ideas.

1. Clitoral stimulation
2. Using your hands while using your tongue.

Clitoral stimulation

Because of the texture of your tongue and your lips, the exploration of her clitoris with either or both of these delivers an exquisitely pleasurable sensation. However, there are a range of ways you can overdo this by applying too much pressure or too much speed to your exploration, particularly if you have been going for a while and her exquisite parts have become incredibly sensitive. So be aware of this as you explore.

But the reality is that because of the musculature of the tongue and lips, with the ranges of softness they bring to the party, you are able to really explore a range of stimulation for her enjoyment. This softness has much more of an impact than that of the finger, so moving from fingers to mouth is a very pleasurable step for her.

Here we are focusing on exploring her clitoris with your tongue, and shortly we will come to working with your lips and mouth.

We have discussed previously that the part of the clitoris we are playing with, at the top of the vulva, has a hood of skin on it. When it is engorged with blood as a result of her being thoroughly turned on, sometimes it will reveal itself out of this hood and sometimes it will still remain hidden. This is going to be very different for everyone you have intimate relations with, as everyone is different in how their body is made.

Starting

Your tongue explorations should be focused on this part of the clitoris, and you can explore this part both with the hood over or the hood gently pulled back revealing the end. Try not to jump into trying to go with maximum stimulation straight away, start with the hood still over and moving your tongue across the clitoris in a range of ways. These will be the same as your finger actions, ranging from side to side, up and down, circles, and mixing these movements up.

When starting in this way, try to explore the whole length of that section of the clitoris as well, don't just focus on the end. This means moving your tongue to the base of it and back and playing with the varying movements as you go. It will feel quite hard on your tongue, which is good as she certainly should be in the midst of fabulous pleasure by now.

While doing this you will be aware of how she is responding by her hip movements, her breathing and any sound she is making. Respond to this. The more practice you have of being tuned in, the better your responses.

If there is something in particular that you are doing, maybe up and down motions, that she is finding particularly exquisite, then keep doing that movement. If she directs you to do something, then as always follow those directions.

Next Steps

Once you have explored stimulating her in this way, you are going to move to reveal more of her by gently moving the hood back. The easiest way to do this is if you touch the skin on her lower abdomen above her vulva and draw it up the body. Obviously, you do this gently without pushing down on her lower belly. Essentially what this does is pulls the skin of the clitoral hood up as well, thus revealing the end of the clitoris in all its glory. It might be that she will do this for you, as it is likely she has done this before in her own pleasure explorations.

So now that the hood is removed you have the glory of 8000 nerve endings to stimulate. There is a significant difference between stimulating the clitoris with the hood over and the hood off. A massive difference. So, start gently as the last thing you want to do is be so overstimulating that you bounce her out of her pleasure.

Continue with the same techniques as before. Up and down action. Side to side actions. Making circles in a variety of different ways. Always listening and aware of the response your actions are making.

It might be that this is too much, then let the hood slip back over and keep going that way, so that the stimulation is toned down. Then when you think it is the right time, draw the hood back and continue.

Mouth and lips action

So far we have been talking about tongue action. But there is also something else you can try with your lips that will up the intensity, so be aware of this as you give it a go.

Draw the hood back so you can place the clitoris between your lips. This end section when appearing out from under the hood is quite little, so this is a delicate little move that requires a little bit of dexterity on the part of your lips. It will fall out or slip out of your lips as you try this, but don't worry if this happens. Just start again.

When you have the clitoris between your lips there are a couple of things to try. Just moving your lips back and forward will result in some intense outcomes. Moving your lips side to side, so that you are essentially 'rolling' your lips over the end of the clit will be quite mind-blowing, as you will be stimulating a significant surface area of it as you go.

You can hold it in your lips and then with your tongue flick the end up and down, side to side or in circles. This is a very small movement, but again the impact is significant. Adding to this particular move is where you suck the clitoris into your mouth at the same time. This can help keep it between your lips, but also the pressure of the sucking action will add to the intensity of feeling you will get.

Finally, and you must be super careful here, you can place the end of the clitoris between your teeth and very gently place pressure on it. Obviously your teeth are a much harder texture than your lips or tongue, so the change in texture becomes very interesting to your partner, and while it is between your teeth you can continue to flick and stroke it with your tongue in a range of ways.

Your turn to explore

The mouth and tongue action described above isn't exhaustive. It isn't meant to be. They are the beginning guidelines to how you can use your tongue and mouth on your partner in ways that massively impact her pleasure. Next we put everything together.

Using your hands as well as your mouth and tongue

By now you will have understood the point of this whole book. How can you have fantastic sex with your partner and really focus on creating maximum extraordinary pleasure for her? And as described in a number of ways above, one of the ways to do this is to have several different actions happening at once.

When you are in the middle of going down on your partner, you will still have your hands available to you to get involved in the pleasure making process.

If you are using one of these hands to draw the skin up to reveal her clitoris, you will still have the other free for fun. And if she is doing this for you, then you have two hands free. You want to be using these hands in a range of ways to ensure she has the best time possible.

With one of your free hands you are going to stimulate her g-spots. This is an opportunity to stimulate not only the g-spot that is on the top of the inside vaginal wall, the 'classic' g-spot, but it is also an opportunity to explore the g-spot that is on the bottom section of the wall as well, and any other position that she responds to in a positive way.

When applying the pressure here, as always, play with varying the pressure until you feel it is right. Don't go in with hard pressure, or pressure that is intense or overpowering. You might start with a soft pressure that gives her time to adjust to the fact that both her clitoris and her g-spot are being stimulated at the same time. Double intensity is pretty full on, so when you start you might think about backing off a little on what you are doing with your tongue and mouth, just so she gets used to it.

Again, don't be doing the porn style fingering, which is fast and furious and pretty aggressive. If that is what she wants you to do, then by all means go for it, but as a default assumption that that is the way forward, don't be doing that action.

Putting it all together

Those are the basic ideas for going down successfully and in such a way that her pleasure is going to be pinging off the charts. Remember that that is what you are working to do, explore all the ways that you can maximise her pleasure while having intimate and glorious sex. When you focus on this, your pleasure will be maximised in return, not only from the feelings you will have from delivering this ecstasy to her, but then what she will do to you in return. It pays dividends but more importantly, your focus on her will draw you deeply into the extraordinary feeling of intimacy.

Penetration

The final bit of the sex puzzle, and possibly the easiest for you to think you know what to do, is the moment where you insert your cock inside her. There are multiple ways for this to happen, multiple positions, multiple everything. We're not going to discuss too much of that here, rather we are going to discuss the other elements that you can explore while inside her, and that will impact what is going on in every position you try.

These include:

1. Body contact or separation

2. The stimulation of her clitoris while inside her
3. Speed or stillness
4. What are your hands and mouth doing?

Body contact or separation?

In the majority of the porn you will have watched, most of the sex you will see will have the man humping and pumping away and almost having no other contact with his partner than his cock. This position is essentially to ensure the cameras can get great shots of his cock going in and out. What it also does is potentially makes it look as though this is how penetration should happen all the time. This is sometimes how it happens but don't think that it is how it should always happen.

For the beginning of this conversation imagine starting in missionary position. You are on top, she is underneath and you are facing each other. In this position, where is the rest of your body? Are you upright and separate? Maybe you are lying directly on top of her, with all of your skin in contact with her skin. Remember, the skin is the biggest organ in the body and when in the middle of deeply pleasurable and intimate sex, those skin nerve endings are firing away from any contact.

Are you kissing her? Are you kissing her neck? Are you stroking her skin, her arms, her breasts, everywhere where that extra contact is going to be stimulating her further? And as you are moving in and out of her, how are you actually doing this, because this is going to create an impact as well?

If you are moving forward and back only, with no other contact around her most exquisite and sensitive areas you are going to be missing a trick. By the way, be careful about pushing her legs back just so you can get in deeper. For some women this can really hurt and it will lead to a very abrupt end to your session.

Stimulation of her clitoris while inside her.

When moving in and out of her, we are still on top here, if you adjust your position and your action so that the front of your pelvis is on hers while you move, you are very likely to be able to also stimulate her clitoris with your movements. You don't want to be forceful with your hip pressure as you move. Like everything else we have discussed in this book it is better to start with softer pressure and move to more than go full on at the beginning.

Another option might be that you are more upright and have less body contact with her as you are moving in and out. This could give you the opportunity to stimulate her with one of your hands. Or if she wants to, she could stimulate herself while you are moving.

On a side note, some guys have the attitude that they don't want their partner to be touching themselves while they are having sex together as it makes them feel as though what they are doing is inadequate.

You should be thinking the opposite of this.

If your partner wants to add their hands and self-stimulation techniques into the mix while you are in the middle of intimate pleasures, encourage them. They are looking to take themselves to incredible places, so help them along.

Whatever your position, whatever you are doing, the amount

of body contact, hand contact and extra stimulation you can provide will vary and will change depending on who you are with, and how each individual is 'feeling it' at that time. Some of your partners might want full body contact all the time. Some might find it stifling, and if there is a big size difference between you, lying on her might make it hard for her to breathe as you are squashing her chest.

Stimulation of her g-spot

In different positions, you may have the opportunity to stimulate her g-spot with the end of your cock as you move inside her, and possibly as you withdraw. This will require some practice and some exploration of different angles from both you and her, and it is definitely something to discuss to try to work out.

This is one of the big bonuses of the reverse cowgirl position, where she is on top of you but facing away from you. With the angle of her position mixed with the general angle of your cock as it is vertical and pointing slightly toward you, the g-spot is touched on nearly every movement.

This is also possible from missionary position, from taking her from behind, literally from every position you try, but some will give you better angles than others.

When in this position and with that g-spot getting regular contact, if you were to add in either yourself or her stimulating her clitoris then you will get a very powerful pleasurable buildup. Definitely worth the experiment and conversation.

Speed or stillness?

One of the great variances you can play with is in mixing up how fast you are going or how slow you are going. Along with the different impacts this kind of variation can bring to your partner's pleasure, variance in speed also gives you control over how long you can sustain what you are doing before you finish.

If you feel like you are close to the edge of finishing and you don't want to yet, then slow down and come to a complete stop if you need to. You can rest for a moment inside her, allow yourself to calm down and desensitise, then start again. On the other hand, if you want to finish then go right ahead.

Alternatively, sometimes you might feel that you want a little more stimulation for yourself because you have been going slowly, so picking up the speed and rhythm can give you that.

The reality is that knowing when and how to change speed while in the middle of a deeply involving, exquisitely intense intimate session with your partner takes practice.

You might have heard about or read about a form of sex called tantric sex. We aren't going to discuss that in this book, however one of the elements of tantric sex is that you stop your movement while you are as deep inside her as you can.

The connection you will feel with your partner when you do this is exquisite, both for you and her. You don't need to stop for very long, a couple of seconds if you want to, but you could stop for longer if you also want to explore what that feels like.

And before you start up again, there is something else you can do while this deep inside her. Just move your hips in very small ways, so you are moving your pelvis against hers, potentially rubbing against the clitoris, but more than anything else applying that pelvic pressure across her whole vulva area. Because a significant part of the clitoris is quite close to the surface of the skin, and by now the whole organ will be stimulated and full of blood, it might be that this movement across all of her will engage and stimulate a significant percentage of it.

What are your hands and your mouth doing?

In all of these adventures in positions, angles and speed the last element to explore is what your hands are doing and your mouth is doing.

It might be that you are so involved in the feeling and intimacy of skin contact as you are having an extraordinary time together and you forget that your hands are also there as a tool for extra stimulation. This extra stimulation won't just impact her. When you are in the middle of an amazing sexual liaison, that contact on your hands of her skin will feel incredible for you as well.

Can you stroke her skin, kiss her neck, apply pressure to her hips. Just adding something extra to her and your sensations will elevate what you have been doing and will give you even more profound intimate sensations.

As with everything you have read about in this book, when you are layering the extra feelings and contact or kissing, go slowly to start with and don't be overwhelming with what you are doing.

Other positions are available

As I am sure you are well aware, there are a significant range of different positions you can try while having fabulous sex with your partner. You will no doubt have seen all of the possibilities from your range of porn watching.

I'm not going to give you a guide on how to go about making the best of each and every one of these positions. That is going to be up to you to find out about. The rules of each one of these positions are the same as the rules for everything you have been reading.

Is it Consensual? Is it Safe?

Some things to consider with these questions. Sometimes your partner just won't want to have you entering her from behind. Sometimes you might not want to be on your back. Sometimes an attempt at a reverse cowgirl by your partner, if she is a little too far down your hips, might be causing your cock to bend in a way that isn't very pleasurable. Maybe you are giving her oral sex and you are on your back and she is on her knees and the pressure from her pelvis and hips means you can't breathe. Maybe you are standing up in the shower and your height difference means the angle of entry is uncomfortable for either or both of you.

You get the idea here. There are many ways of exploring each other but there are also many variables that you just have to be open about respecting if it isn't working for you or for her.

This difficulties in positions, where you can't breathe,

or it just isn't working or it is a bit uncomfortable is a brilliant opportunity to have a laugh about what you are doing. Sometimes, the uncomfortable position, or the trying to get comfortable in an uncomfortable position, can be very funny. I often think there are two ways this can go. You can get frustrated, or you can get amused. Don't get frustrated. Get amused. Enjoy the humour of it.

When you have finished

We discussed a couple of times earlier in this book that just because you have finished doesn't necessarily mean that the sex you have been having has finished.

Sometimes it is finished. Sometimes you finishing will be at the end of an hour or more of exploration, pleasure and mind-blowing intimacy. And you finishing is the end. She might have reached her peak, maybe she is getting to the point where the friction of you inside her is just diminishing in pleasure. Lots of reasons. You finish, you both finish.

But often if you have finished, she won't have. And a lot of the narrative of these situations is that she is left high and dry, on the way to her peak and her pleasure, and you are done and it all stops. A deeply frustrating situation and if that happens on a regular basis then it becomes a challenge to want to have sex with you because the pleasure of the experience is only really felt by you and not her.

So then one of the habits to get into, and it is a habit and a practice, is to keep going with your hands and mouth when you have finished. The sooner into your sexual adventures you do this, the better it will be for you and your partners. This is because if you have spent several years finishing when you finish, then this might be a challenge of a habit to break for you.

When you have finished and keep your partner going, what do you do? All that you have read about so far. Using your hands, using your mouth, slowing down, speeding up, friction on the skin, kissing. Everything you have done before, but now she is in the middle of extreme pleasure and your sole focus is on taking her into places where it will just get better and better for her.

You will know when to stop or she will tell you when she has had enough. Again, this will take some practice to be able to read the signs and to understand when the time is right. And when she has had enough, she will make it clear to you.

There is also the option that, while you might have both 'finished' in terms of the intense sexual experience you have both shared, you still stroke her skin, hold onto her, kiss her, keep the contact going in whatever way you feel like. This post-sex gentle touching, talking, kissing can feel amazing, and while your and her nerves are still tingling and your and her skin is still incredibly responsive to the lightest of touches, you find a way to wind down your experience together. This isn't necessarily every time you have sex with someone, but you will probably find that the more you enjoy intimate encounters with someone, the more you will enjoy a calming down of senses together in this way.

The opposite is sometimes true, where as soon as you are finished you want to be somewhere else.

After you are properly finished

So what happens when you are truly finished. All the intimate explorations are done, your final wind down is done, or not, and then what happens? You need to dispose of your condom properly. Tie a knot in the end so there is no spillage and bin it, not down a toilet, but in a bin. You might wrap it in toilet paper if you need to cover it, or wrap it in toilet paper, take it with your wherever you are going and dispose of it somewhere else.

Leaving someone as quickly as possible after an intimate encounter can be pretty humiliating for the person you are leaving. But on the opposite side of that, sometimes the person you are with might want you gone as they don't want to spend the rest of the night with you.

The biggest rule here is, don't be an asshole, but also don't overstay your welcome. Maybe you are at yours, and you don't want her to stay the night. Again, don't be an asshole.

Do you want to see her again? Does she want to see you again? Ghosting someone after you have slept with them once is a dick move, so don't ghost someone, even if you don't want to see them again. Be respectful and tell them. If it gets challenging and problematic, then blocking is always an option, but open communication should stop that becoming a necessity.

If you do want to see her again, make sure she knows. She can't read your mind, and you can't read hers. It might be that you want to see her and she doesn't want to see you. This can and will happen. One of life's guarantees is that when you embark on relationship journeys, your heart will be broken and you will be responsible for breaking the heart of others.

As long as you understand this, the heart break, or responsibility for others, will be easier to deal with. It won't be painless. Just less of a surprise.

And if she wants to see you but you don't want to see her, be gentle and be kind. But also, be straightforward. Don't speak in riddles that might be misunderstood. She might be upset at you initially, but it is better to be clear than to tag someone along because you are scared of hurting them.

When you embark on these journeys into intimacy and relationships all the world's emotions will be thrown at you, the positive and the negative. This is part of the joy of life, but the secret of it is that the positives always outweigh the negatives.

70

Conclusion

Sex is amazing and incredible and intimate and profound and wonderful. Sex can also be a challenge to your ego, self-centred and a power game.

This whole book has been about how you in your future sexual adventures can explore sex as the incredible, intimate wonder that it is, not the self-centred power game it can be.

Your pursuit in this exploration of sex is her pleasure. Your role is to ensure that you do all you can do to give her the most extraordinary and pleasure filled time. If this is your focus, then your pleasure will hit similar heights. You have to trust this is true. If you focus on her pleasure, then your pleasure will be incredible.

Talk to your partner, ask her what she likes and ask her to tell you if you are doing something that she doesn't like. There is enormous pressure on women to not tell you about something that isn't pleasurable, and to just put up with something that doesn't feel very nice. Ensure she feels she can tell you and when she does, follow her requests as quickly as you can.

This is your opportunity to write your sexual and intimate

future yourself, not have it written for you by adults and media who are shaming you and who are expecting you to assault everyone you have sex with.

The future is in your hands and the future can be an incredible and pleasure filled sexual paradise, but you have to work for it, you have to be responsible for it and it will take time and patience.

Take responsibility for talking with your friends about this book and about the ways they engage with intimacy. You don't have to go into details. I write in section 1 about how talking about your experiences isn't a good idea, but you can help guide your friends if you think they are going down the wrong path.

Sex is amazing and incredible and intimate and you can have the most extraordinary sexual life. Focus on your partner's pleasure. Focus on listening to them and on sharing this sexual adventure with them.

It is all up to you. You can do it.

Appendix: Exercises for better sensitivity and skill

Whoever did something brilliantly the first time they did it? Everyone sucks the first time they try a new thing, whether it is a sport, learning a new skill, or sex. So the reality is the first time you have sex, you're not going to be particularly good. This is just the reality.

But if you are able to bring together skills you have practiced, with an increased understanding of what you are feeling under your fingertips, then maybe the first time you won't suck too much. And if you are already being intimate, then these exercises will massively improve your skills and your abilities to create pleasurable experiences for you both.

And this is what this section is about. This section is about developing some basic understandings of touch and sensitivity in your fingertips and some coordination exercises so when you are getting intimate with someone you have some physical skills already available to you.

When being intimate you want your touch to be sensitive and responsive to your partner and you want to be able to do a couple of different actions at the same time.

The exercises in the next several pages are a combination of strength and sensitivity exercises, and all are designed to help you be better at your own actions of intimacy as well as being better in terms of what you feel and how you feel it through your fingertips

Never forget we are always capable of learning more. And these exercises form a part of this constant learning. You can always be practicing to make your touch more aware of sensation. You can always explore new ways of feeling her heartbeat through her skin. You can always work your core muscles to ensure when you are in the middle of intimate connections you are strong and supple with your actions, not floppy and weak with your core and not broken after a bit of action that is more active than you might have anticipated.

This is probably a good point to talk briefly about strength and fitness and the impact this will have on your intimate adventures. The is a big generalisation, but the fitter you are, the more fun you are going to have. Being fitter will give you more stamina to be able to pay attention to your partner. Strength will give you a better structure for more interesting positions to explore. Ultimately, as you become fitter and stronger, you will become more aware of your body. This is called proprioception. An increase in awareness brings with it an increase in feeling pleasure across your whole body.

Hand exercises and coordination skills (doing two or three things at once)

Hand Exercises

The exercises in this section focus on the sensitivity and strength in your hands and specifically an awareness of sensitivity for what is underneath your fingertips and sensitivity to the pressure you are exerting to find that sensitivity.

If you are looking to spend time stroking your partner's clitoris, you need to be able to feel what you are doing and react accordingly, go slower or faster, more pressure or less pressure, to ensure she is flying and in delirious ecstasy.

Doing these exercises will mean you aren't going to be Mr Fumbly and feel to your partner like some noob who has no idea what they are doing. True and repeatable physical satisfaction of your partner involves an awareness of what is going on underneath your fingertips and then knowing how to respond to that awareness.

Sometimes you will require a touch so light it can hardly be felt, but will feel like maximum pressure to your partner. At other times your touch will need to be stronger and less delicate.

These choices will be made by you. You can only begin to make these choices when you have the skills to do so and the awareness to know what you are feeling and the range of actions that can respond to those feelings.

When you do these exercises you will begin to get a feel for what different surfaces feel like and will be able to pick up very small changes in the different surfaces you are feeling. This will translate to your intimate experiences and will translate to the impact your touch will have on your partner. As you develop more awareness of your touch on flat surfaces, play with touching different clothing materials, and different metal surfaces. Having an array of different materials to work with will improve your awareness and response.

Exercise beginning

1.Splay your fingers out onto a table or flat surface to create a 'spider' hand. Contract your fingers so the back of your hand moves toward the ceiling. Slowly lower the palm of the hand back toward the surface. Work with the idea you are squeezing your hand inward.

Vary the speed of movement as you are moving your hand and vary the amount of pressure you are feeling through your fingers. Try doing the same movement and pressure as you lower the palm back toward the surface.

Do this same exercise, but with one finger at a time, so for example you might have your palm flat, then lift your middle fingers and only contract the thumb and little finger to raise your palm.

Remember you are trying to 'feel' what is happening underneath your fingertips. You are working to increase the sensation of the pressure on the table as your hand slides along it.

2. Place the palm of your hand on the surface of a table with your thumb sitting on the edge. Drag your fingers toward the edge using your thumb as a fulcrum. Once you have got to the edge of the table with your fingers, push them back along the table.

With the same process as the first exercise, ensure you vary your speed of movement and pressure. Sometimes work with a very light touch and sometimes increase the pressure to as much as possible.

Then work with one finger at a time, or two, but change the two you use, and in particular, if there is a combination you are finding difficult, or it feels like a weird and uncomfortable coordination, then keep repeating that movement. For example, if you have your little finger and middle finger on the surface and your index and ring finger in the air, it might feel unusual. Repeat the ones that feel the strangest.

3. Hold your hand with the palm on the table and your fingers in the air. In sequence tap your little finger, ring finger, middle finger, index finger and then thumb on the table. Start slowly and try to have a steady rhythm to what you are doing. Work up the speed of tapping until you have a fast and steady beat.

When you are feeling comfortable with going from the little finger to the thumb, reverse the sequence so you start at the thumb then work back to your little finger.

Do the sequence with one hand at a time then with both hands at a time. When working with both hands, start with both hands going from the little finger to the thumb, then both hands going from the thumb to the little finger. When you are feeling like this is getting easier, change the sequence so when you start at your little finger on your left hand, you also start with your thumb on the right, then reverse it so you start with the right little finger and the left thumb.

For the most challenging of coordination, start different hands with different fingers, but put one finger down on each hand at exactly the same time. For example, start with your left hand ring finger and your right hand thumb. When in this sequence, your last finger to touch down will be your little finger on your left hand and your little finger on your right. Start slow, keep changing the starting point and see how you can build your coordination abilities.

This double handed exercise, particularly when you are

going in the same direction, therefore starting with different fingers, is brilliant for training you to be able to coordinate your touch and your hands to be doing different things at the same time. This is the type of multi-skilled ability we need.

4. Do the exercises above with your fingers long and out-stretched and then in all the positions up to and including the position where your palm is still on the table but your fingers are as vertical as they can be.

5. Find a flat surface that also has a raised or lowered line in it, like a seam or a join. Drag your finger along it to discover what your sense of touch is like. Try it with each of your fingers. Use both hands.

Now do the same exercise along a seam and vary the amount of pressure you are applying. Push as hard as you can, then touch it as lightly as you possibly can. Find different amounts of positive pressure as you push as hard as possible. Can you get a sense of when you are at about 50% of maximum pressure? What does it feel like? Remember, you are doing this while trying to feel the seam or line you are on. Now do the same going the other way, so get lighter and lighter with your touch until you can't touch any more.

There are a couple of reasons to do this particular variance in pressure. For a lot of guys, when it comes to touch there is either 'On' or "Off".

Sometimes when you are applying pressure or gripping with your hands or fingers and you are in the middle of a fabulous session with your partner you can grip too hard and leave bruises. You won't mean to do it, and she may well not even notice at the time, but afterwards it might make you feel like you lost a bit of control. So if you are able to vary your grip/pressure of contact so you are much more in control and aware, then the better for both of you.

Conversely, sometimes she will want a much lighter touch, and you need to be able to help her without it being so light she can't feel it or so it becomes ticklish, which can just be annoying. Lighten up your contact abilities so she gets what she is asking for. And sometimes extraordinarily light, particularly when getting your hands involved in her intimate places, is the only contact that is possible because she has become so wonderfully sensitive she can't take any other touch.

6. Now repeat the exercise and the pressure variations on another surface. The more you drag your fingers and explore sensation, the greater your awareness of surface sensitivity will become.

7. Run your fingers down the edge of a door or wall, keeping your finger clearly on the edge and following the same line.

So remember that with all of these exercises, vary the amount of pressure exerted. This is purely so you can see what is most comfortable and also how much pressure is required for the most sensitivity. An awareness of surface changes across all pressures is what we are looking for. An additional exercise is to place your hand on different appliances while they are working, just to find the feel of different vibrations under your hand.

If you place your hand on the side of your refrigerator when it is on, then you will undoubtedly feel the vibration of the motor moving through the surface. Move your hand around the surface of the fridge and find where the vibration is more or is less. Get a feel for the change in tone of the vibration, of the varying intensity of it and begin to work with feeling the vibration as soon as you touch the surface, rather than waiting.

Try the same exercise with other appliances, for example, your shower head will normally be vibrating due to the water coursing through it. Put your hand on this and feel the vibration through the surface. Adjust the volume of water coming through it and feel the difference in vibration as it happens.

Pelvic floor

The muscles of the pelvic floor are fascinating. They are a sling of muscles supporting the bladder and bowel as well as giving you control over your bladder when you are busting to go, and over your farts when you are in a situation where releasing a killer is going to make you a social pariah.

The muscles of the pelvic floor are also very helpful for your sex life. Most of the conversations regarding sex and pelvic floor muscles are geared towards women, but they can make a rather fantastic difference to us blokes if we use them well. Also, the exercising of them supports the lower core structures of your torso and the link between your torso, pelvis and legs, so may make you stronger as well.

1.Can you stop yourself peeing mid-flow? This is a very simple exercise to do, but not one you want to do too much of, as there are risks of bladder infections if you do it too much. Very simply, when you are having a pee, engage those muscles that stop the flow from happening. I advise you here to not stop yourself totally, but perhaps at about 50% of flow volume. You might feel contractions happening down your legs and into your stomach. This is fine, the exercise is merely to give you the beginning of an understanding of how you use your pelvic floor.

Every time you pee, slow down and speed up your flow by contracting these muscles. Also don't just turn them on or off. Explore different percentages of on and off, explore how you can slow down and then speed up the flow as you go. You don't want just on and off, you want to work with the whole range of effort with these muscles.

2.Now you have the awareness and the beginning of a range of controls, it is time to start exercising them.

Sitting comfortably to start with, try to engage your pelvic floor muscles in isolation. Contract your front ones (the stop peeing ones) without contracting the back ones (the stopping you farting ones). And also try to contract these without contracting the muscles in your legs or stomach.

As you are doing this you will realise contracting one without the other is quite challenging, but keep trying. So you might isolate the back pelvic floor muscles without engaging the front, or vice versa. Don't do what most people do and practice the easiest one so it makes you feel more accomplished. Practice the one that is the hardest to do.

3.Now in isolation and all together, there are two very basic exercises to do. Contract both muscles slowly (over a period of about 5 seconds) then release over the same time frame. Do about 5 of these.

Now contract super quickly, and release just as quickly. About 6 of these in a row, then rest. Now with isolation and with all together, this should give you a range of options. You should be able to begin to do these exercises standing up, sitting down, walking and moving. Keep trying, keep working different muscles, keep exploring how you can isolate them. Just remember, don't do it too hard or you might irritate your system, which isn't a nice feeling.

Coordination exercises & what can your non-dominant hand do?

Having now trained your techniques and skills with your hands, you now need to explore how you can work compe-tently with both hands at the same time. After all, with the new era of intimacy we have been talking about throughout the book, the more skills and options you have available to you and the more you are able to confidently make these work, the happier you and especially your partner will be.

Can you do two different things with each of your hands at the same time? A couple of things to try.

1.On a table draw circles in opposite directions with your hands/fingers. Start with keeping the circles the same size, then increase the size of one without increasing the size of the other, then slowly reverse so the smaller circle becomes large and the large small.

Move your hands so they are not directly in front of you, but one arm is long so the circle is further away and the other arm bent so that circle is closer. Remember that all of these exercises are also opportunities for further explorations of sensations under the fingers.

2.Now explore different actions of your hands. With one hand draw circles on a desk and with the other hand draw straight lines. Swap roles across your hands, so if you are circling with the left, start circling with the right.

Once you feel like you have this, change the direction of the straight lines, and change the size of the circles. And once you have this, change the size of the lines, but also change the speed of each of your hands as well.

Remember, whoever did something brilliantly the first time they did it? Everyone sucks the first time they try a new thing, whether it is a sport, a skill, or sex. You're not going to be particularly good. This is just the reality.

But if you are able to bring together skills you have multi-skilled, with an increased understanding of what you are feeling under your fingertips, then maybe the first time you won't suck too much.

If by your preparation your partner has a clear indication you are focused on making your intimate sessions as incredible for her as possible, then I promise you she will be wanting to reciprocate and you will have a brilliant time together.

About the Author

Ben Dunks is a artist, educator and writer who has spent a significant portion of his adult life working with young people of all ages and in all settings. Most of this time this has been in Dance and Education but he has also spent time as a massage therapist, immersive technologist, sports pants designer and writer of everything from articles to education programmes, funding applications and now books about intimacy and sex.

Ben is deeply passionate about movement, creativity and the expressions of our identity through creativity. Ben is also deeply passionate about exploring subjects that are 'difficult', or that are still surrounded by the idea of being 'difficult' because they create embarrassment, push against religious traditions or just make us uncomfortable.

He also believes that if you think you have a part of a solution for a problem that is much bigger than any one individual can solve, then it is your responsibility to put that solution into the world. That is what Intimacy is. This is Ben's partial solution to a problem that is going to take a whole host of organisations and individuals to come together to solve.

Ben is Australian but has been living in the UK for over 20 years. He can be contacted at www.benjamindunks.com.

Thank you

I couldn't have written this without the incredible support of my amazing wife Nix. The framing and the voice of this book is primarily down to her careful and patient reading and responding to many many drafts over five years. You are wonderful. Thank you.

The first proper proof was done by Cherish Amber, a Sex Therapist, Podcaster, friend and colleague and who is changing the world. Thank you.

The book cover and illustrations are by Amber Hope Evans. I am sure you love them as much as we do. That cover is incredible. Thank you.

To the Mums and friends who read it, commented and challenged it, a massive thank you. One of my very early desires was that the book would be mum approved. It has been. Goal achieved.

Bibliography

Bibliography

Anand, Margo. *The art of sexual ecstasy*. London. Thorsons.

Biddulph, Steve. *Manhood*. Sydney. Random House.

Biddulph, Steve. *Raising Boys*. London. Thorsons.

Chia, Mantak. Chia, Maneewan. Abrams, Douglas. Rachel Carlton Abrams. *Multi-Orgasmic Couple*. London. Thorsons.

Chia, Mantak. The Multi-orgasmic man. London. Thorsons.

Connell, R. W. *Masculinities*. Cambridge. Blackwell Publishers Ltd.

Corinna, Heather. *s.e.x. the all-you-need-to-know sexuality guide to get you through your teens and twenties.* Boston: Da Capo Press.

Frederick, David, Kate St.John, H, Garcia, Justin & Lloyd, Elisabeth. *Differences in Orgasm Frequency among Gay, Lesbian, Bisexual, and Heterosexual Men and Women in a US National Sample*. Archives of Sexual Behavior 47, 273-288.

Friday, Nancy. *Men in Love*. London. Arrow Books Ltd.

Friday, Nancy. *My Secret Garden*. London. Quartet Books

Friday, Nancy. *Women on Top*. London. Hutchinson.

Fulbright, Yvonne. *His Guide to Going Down*. New York. Adams Media.

Kerner, Ian. *She Comes First*. London. Souvenir Press.

Kontula, Osmo. Miettinen, Anneli. *Determinants of female sexual orgasms*. Socioeffective Neuroscience & Psychology 2016. (Orgasm: Neurophysiological, psychological, and evolutionary perspectives)

Nagoski, Emily. *Come as you are*. Rev. ed. London: Scribe Publications.

Orenstein, Peggy. *Boys and Sex*. New York. Harper Collins.

Richardson, Diana. *Tantric Orgasm for Women*. Rochester. Destiny Books.

Printed in Great Britain
by Amazon

29373425R10129